Advance Praise for *Welfare, Work, and Poverty* by Qin Gao

Welfare, Work, and Poverty

International Policy Exchange Series

Published in collaboration with the
Center for International Policy Exchanges
University of Maryland

Series Editors
Douglas J. Besharov
Neil Gilbert

SCHOOL of
PUBLIC POLICY

WELFARE, WORK, AND POVERTY

Social Assistance in China

QIN GAO

OXFORD
UNIVERSITY PRESS

OXFORD
UNIVERSITY PRESS

Oxford University Press is a department of the University of Oxford. It furthers
the University's objective of excellence in research, scholarship, and education
by publishing worldwide. Oxford is a registered trade mark of Oxford University
Press in the UK and certain other countries.

Published in the United States of America by Oxford University Press
198 Madison Avenue, New York, NY 10016, United States of America.

Library of Congress Cataloging-in-Publication Data
Names: Gao, Qin, 1977– author.
Title: Welfare, work, and poverty : social assistance in China / Qin Gao.
Description: New York : Oxford University Press, [2017] |
Includes bibliographical references.
Identifiers: LCCN 2016040535 (print) | LCCN 2016051799 (ebook) |
ISBN 9780190218133 (alk. paper) | ISBN 9780190218140
Subjects: LCSH: Public welfare—China. | China—Social policy.
Classification: LCC HV418 .G3626 2017 (print) | LCC HV418 (ebook) |
DDC 362.5/80951—dc23
LC record available at https://lccn.loc.gov/2016040535

9 8 7 6 5 4 3 2 1

Printed by Sheridan Books, Inc., United States of America

In memory of my grandparents
and
for my parents,
who taught me all about
compassion, hard work, and dignity

CONTENTS

LIST OF TABLES AND FIGURES

TABLES

FIGURES

Welfare, Work, and Poverty

1

INTRODUCTION

WELFARE, WORK, AND POVERTY: THE CHINESE CASE

Poverty in China has dropped sharply since the market-oriented economic reforms were launched in the late 1970s. Yet alongside this phenomenal achievement, unemployment in urban areas and rising income inequality nationwide emerged (Gustafsson, Sicular, & Li, 2008; Khan & Riskin, 2001, 2005; Li, Sato, & Sicular, 2013; Riskin, Zhao, & Li, 2001). The traditional social assistance program during the planned-economy period in urban China, which aimed at helping the group of "Three Withouts" (i.e., those without income source, ability to work, or a legal guardian or supporter), was small in scale and excluded able-bodied unemployed persons. The combination of unemployment and growing income inequality created the urgent need to develop a broader social assistance program that could serve as a last resort for the very poor.

China's market-based economic reforms changed the previous "iron rice bowl," which guaranteed work with low wages in urban areas but also generous and comprehensive social security to a hierarchical and fragmented labor market. Those with stronger political and social ties and greater skills survived and thrived in the labor market, while those with less advantageous backgrounds were left behind. Furthermore, the post-reform Chinese social welfare system is largely regressive in nature, with those with better jobs and at higher positions receiving much better social benefits (Croll, 1999; Davis, 1989; Leung, 2003; Saunders & Shang, 2001; Tang, 2004; Tang, Sha, & Ren, 2003). A survey in 2013 showed that low-income urban families paid for 72% of their medical expenses out of pocket, while that percentage was 50% for middle- and high-income families (Wang, 2013).

China's market-economic reforms and simultaneous social policy reforms have left the urban poor behind. On the one hand, many of the new urban poor had few skills or bad health to begin with and thus were not competitive in the labor market and received low wages or remained unemployed. On the other hand, social policy reforms shifted the responsibility of social insurance from employers, especially state-owned enterprises (SOEs), to be shared among employers, employees, and the government. In this process, the previous largely equally distributed social benefits became more closely tied to a person's employment status, sector, and position. Those who had less stable and lower-ranked jobs suffered most, losing many of their social benefits and having to contribute a relatively large proportion of their income to social insurance.

As a result, the social welfare system as a whole actually worked to enlarge the market income gaps and functioned as a de facto regressive force, as evident in Gao and Riskin's (2009) detailed decomposition analysis of income inequality. Using national household survey data, they found that all of the major social benefit categories, including pensions, health insurance, housing, and food, played a disequalizing role, lifting the relative positions of the rich and lowering those of the poor. The only solution to shield the poor from material desolation and political upheaval was to provide social assistance that could serve as a basic safety net. Their empirical evidence showed that social assistance was the only equalizing social benefit that helped lift the relative position of the poor.

It is against this backdrop that this book focuses on the Minimum Livelihood Guarantee (MLG, or *Dibao*), China's primary social assistance program that aims to provide a basic safety net for the poor in both urban and rural areas and ensure social and political stability. More than 20 years after the introduction of Dibao, this book provides the first systematic and comprehensive evaluation in English of its impact and effectiveness and offers timely policy implications regarding its future.

Specifically, the book addresses the following questions. How effective has Dibao been in targeting the poor and alleviating poverty? Have Dibao recipients been dependent on welfare, or have they been able to move from welfare to work? How has Dibao affected their consumption patterns and subjective well-being? Do they use the Dibao subsidy to meet survival needs (such as food, clothing, and shelter) or invest in human capital (such as health and education)? Are they distressed by the stigma associated with receiving Dibao, or do they become more optimistic about the future and enjoy greater satisfaction in life because of the Dibao support? And, finally, what policy lessons can we learn from the existing evidence to strengthen and improve Dibao in the future?

SOCIAL ASSISTANCE IN CHINA: DIBAO AND ITS SUPPLEMENTARY PROGRAMS

China's primary social assistance program, Dibao, was introduced in 1993 in Shanghai. An anti-poverty safety net program, Dibao was created to tackle rising urban poverty in the early 1990s and was implemented nationwide in urban areas in 1999. Since then, it has undergone significant expansions in its coverage and benefits, becoming the dominant social assistance program in China and functioning as a progressive redistributive force. Building on this urban experience, Dibao was implemented nationwide in rural areas in 2007, partly to address the growing urban–rural gap in living standards and the alarmingly lagging conditions of social welfare in rural China.

Dibao is a centrally regulated and locally implemented program. Initiated as a local policy in Shanghai, Dibao is largely financed by local governments and subsidized by the central government when local governments have financial difficulties. For cities and counties in less developed areas, the subsidies from the central government can be substantial, but the responsibility for implementing and sustaining Dibao remains that of local governments. The central government monitors and regulates Dibao through the Department of Social Assistance of the Ministry of Civil Affairs (MCA) and its local subordinates. In a remarkably transparent fashion that distinguishes itself from many other government departments, MCA has consistently published Dibao data on its website, providing a valuable resource for policy researchers as well as the public.

Judged in terms of both total expenditures and the number of beneficiaries, Dibao is the largest social assistance program in China. In the last quarter of 2014, as shown in Table 1.1, total Dibao expenditures accounted for over three quarters of national social assistance expenditures. The rural Dibao expenditure was 42.0% of national social assistance expenditures, amounting to 84.4 billion

Table 1.1. Expenditures for China's Main Social Assistance Programs, Fourth Quarter of 2014

Program	Expenditure (billion yuan)	%
Rural Dibao	84.4	42.0
Urban Dibao	69.5	34.6
Medical Assistance	22.9	11.4
Rural Wubao	18.8	9.4
Other	5.4	2.7
TOTAL	201.0	100.0

Source: Ministry of Civil Affairs (2015b). Quarterly Statistical Report on Social Services (fourth quarter of 2014), http://files2.mca.gov.cn/cws/201501/20150129172531166.htm, accessed April 4, 2015.

yuan, while the urban Dibao expenditure was 34.6%, or 69.5 billion yuan. By the end of 2014, as shown in Table 1.2, the number of urban Dibao beneficiaries reached 18.8 million, representing 2.5% of the urban population. The number of rural Dibao beneficiaries was 52.1 million, or 8.4% of the rural population. Indeed, measured by the number of beneficiaries, Dibao is currently the world's largest social assistance program.

Dibao is supplemented by an array of other social assistance programs, some of which are more closely linked to Dibao than others. Two traditional social assistance programs, one for urban residents and one for rural residents, have existed since the early stages of the socialist regime, targeting the "old poor," or those who lack the ability to work and family support. Dibao, along with a set of other supplementary programs—including education, medical, housing, and temporary assistance—have been set up to provide support to the "new poor," who may have the ability to work but are still unable to meet basic living needs. Many of the new poor are victims of the economic reforms that have transformed the Chinese economy into a much more competitive one, favoring those fit to survive and thrive in a market economy.

The two traditional social assistance programs set up during the 1950s— "Three Withouts" (*Sanwu*) in urban areas and "Five Guarantees" (*Wubao*) in rural areas—target the most vulnerable groups in society and function as the last resort for people in need. The assumption behind these programs is that family, extended kin, and communities are responsible for helping take care of those who are unable to support themselves, and only in extreme cases should the government step in to provide social assistance to the very disadvantaged.

In particular, the Sanwu program provides basic livelihood support to urban residents who have no source of income, ability to work, or family support. The majority of the Sanwu beneficiaries are older people; a small proportion are children and those with physical disability or mental illness. The Wubao program targets rural residents who are old, vulnerable, orphaned, widowed, or disabled (*lao ruo gu gua can*) and who have no ability to work or no family support. It provides financial assistance to meet five aspects of their basic needs, including food, clothing, shelter, medical care, and burial. Children who qualify for Wubao are also guaranteed education assistance. Some Sanwu and Wubao beneficiaries receive cash and in-kind supports at their own homes, while others receive support in collective living arrangements—mostly senior centers set up and maintained by the local government or collective.

Since the implementation of urban Dibao, the beneficiaries of the Sanwu program have been gradually absorbed into the Dibao system. By the end of 2014, the Sanwu group reached 0.5 million, accounting for 3% of all urban Dibao recipients. Typically, Sanwu recipients are entitled to the full Dibao benefit amount prescribed by the local government since they have no source of income,

Table 1.2. Number of Beneficiaries and Per Capita Expenditures of China's Main Social Assistance Programs, Fourth Quarter of 2014

Program	Number of Beneficiaries (million persons)	Per Capita Expenditure (monthly yuan)
Urban Dibao	18.8	274.6
Rural Dibao	52.1	125.3
Rural Wubao—living at home or with relatives	3.5	250.9
Rural Wubao—collective living arrangements	1.7	354.3

Source: Ministry of Civil Affairs (2015b). Quarterly Statistical Report on Social Services (fourth quarter of 2014), http://files2.mca.gov.cn/cws/201501/20150129172531166.htm, accessed April 4, 2015.

whereas other Dibao recipients are only entitled to the difference between the local Dibao assistance standard (also known as Dibao line or threshold) and their income.

In contrast, the Wubao program in rural areas is still administered separately from the rural Dibao, given the short history of rural Dibao's national implementation. As shown in Table 1.2, in the last quarter of 2014, the total number of Wubao beneficiaries was 5.2 million, corresponding to approximately 10% of the rural Dibao recipients. Among them, about two thirds lived in their own homes or with relatives and received an average monthly subsidy of 251 yuan, while the other one third were housed in collective living arrangements, with an average monthly expenditure of 354 yuan per beneficiary.

In addition to the traditional Sanwu and Wubao programs, Dibao is supplemented by several other social assistance programs that were implemented more recently to help address the unique needs of certain subpopulations among the poor. These programs provide housing, medical, education, and temporary assistance (Liu, 2010). Table 1.3 details the key features of these supplemental programs, including their year of enactment, funding sources, target population, and forms of assistance. Unfortunately, data on the number of beneficiaries and the average level of benefits for these programs are not available.

Among these supplementary programs, housing assistance was first established in urban areas in 1999 to provide low-rent housing to poor families with severe housing needs. In 2007, this program was further expanded to provide cash subsidies for rent in urban areas. In rural areas, most families can build their own housing. The government gives priority to offering support for renovation of shabby or dangerous housing of poor families in rural areas. The Ministries of Civil Affairs, Finance, and Housing and Urban-Rural Development administer this program together, and the central and local governments fund this program jointly.

Table 1.3. Social Assistance Programs Supplementary to Dibao

Program	Year Launched and Entity	Funding Source	Target Population	Form of Assistance
Housing Assistance	1999 (low-rent housing), 2007 (cash subsidy for rent), Ministries of Civil Affairs, Finance, and Housing and Urban-Rural Development	Central and local governments	Urban Dibao and other families with severe housing needs, and rural families in shabby or dangerous housing conditions	1) Low-rent housing and cash subsidy for rent in urban areas 2) Priority for renovation of shabby or dangerous housing in rural areas
Medical Assistance	2003 (rural), 2005 (urban), and 2009 (national), Ministries of Civil Affairs, Health, and Finance	Local governments, supplemented by the central government	Dibao and Wubao families as well as families with financial difficulty and severe medical needs	Cash subsidies (mostly through reimbursement) in support of paying for health insurance premiums, doctor visits, and inpatient treatments
Education Assistance	2004, Ministries of Civil Affairs and Education	Central and local governments, supplemented by NGOs and social donations	Sanwu, Wubao, and Dibao recipient children and other children deemed eligible by local governments	1) Free compulsory education for Sanwu and Wubao children 2) Tuition and fee waiver and boarding subsidy for Dibao children in compulsory education (liangmian yibu) 3) Subsidy for high school education, if necessary
Temporary Assistance	2007 (initial setup) and 2014 (national policy), Ministry of Civil Affairs	Local governments supplemented by the central government	Individuals and families facing extreme difficulties due to disasters or severe illness; Dibao and other families with urgent needs due to necessary expenses beyond financial capacity	Cash and in-kind subsidies as well as referral for services

Medical assistance was first piloted in rural areas in 2003 and in urban areas in 2005. It was then established nationally in 2009. The Ministries of Civil Affairs, Health, and Finance administer this program jointly. Local governments are primarily responsible for financing this program, with supplemental funds coming from the central government. The target population of medical assistance includes Dibao and Wubao families as well as other families with financial difficulties and severe medical needs. The assistance is provided as cash subsidies— mostly through reimbursements—that pay for health insurance premiums, doctor visits, and inpatient treatments.

Education assistance was launched in 2004 jointly by the Ministries of Civil Affairs and Education. Both the central and local governments provide funding for this program, supplemented by funds from non-governmental organizations (NGOs) that specialize in offering education support as well as social donations. The target population includes children of Sanwu, Wubao, and Dibao families and other children deemed eligible by local governments. Education assistance takes three forms in its delivery: free compulsory education for Sanwu and Wubao children; waiver of tuition and fees and provision of boarding subsidies for Dibao children in compulsory education (called "two waivers and one subsidy," or *liangmian yibu*); and subsidies for high school education in situations deemed necessary by local governments.

Temporary assistance, the newest social assistance program in China, was initially set up in 2007 and then launched nationally in 2014. Its goal is to provide urgent and temporary assistance to families and individuals facing sudden, unexpected disasters, incidents, diseases, or other hardships when Dibao and other assistance programs are unable to offer timely or sufficient help. Funding for this program is mainly provided by local governments and supplemented by the central government. Assistance includes cash and in-kind subsidies as well as referrals for other types of assistance and appropriate services.

It is noteworthy that eligibility for nearly all these four types of supplementary assistance programs is tied to Dibao eligibility, making Dibao the de facto gatekeeper for a bundle of social benefits and services. This tied eligibility rule serves as a double-edged sword. On the one hand, it saves additional administrative costs and reinforces targeting performance of social assistance if Dibao eligibility is determined accurately. On the other hand, the determination of Dibao eligibility clearly carries too much weight. It may deter families from leaving Dibao even when they are able to do so, for fear that they may lose eligibility for other benefits altogether. It may also increase mis-targeting of the various benefits involved when Dibao eligibility is determined inaccurately.

Based on a survey of 2,811 Dibao households in three cities (Jinan, Changsha, and Baotou) in 2012, Xu (2013) reported that 34% of these Dibao households received education assistance, 22% received housing assistance, and 9% received medical assistance. Among those who received housing assistance, 60% received cash subsidies for rent, 31% lived in low-rent housing, and 9% received other housing support. Because the eligibility for most of these supplemental benefits was tied to Dibao eligibility, it is not surprising that nearly half (46%) of the respondents rated Dibao as the most important benefit, followed by medical assistance (10%), housing assistance (6%), and education assistance (5%). The other 33% of the respondents considered all of these benefits equally important.

VALUES AND PRINCIPLES

Four core values and principles guide the design, implementation, and development of China's social assistance programs, particularly Dibao. These values and principles are deeply rooted in China's ancient history as well as the more recent but powerful socialist regime. First and foremost, following Confucian tradition, the role of *family and community* has been central in managing livelihood and providing support in the Chinese society. It is not only one's own responsibility to earn a living. Family members, extended kin, and the community are also responsible for offering help to those suffering hardship. As a result, throughout Chinese history, support for the poor has been handled primarily within the family, extended kin, and community, while obtaining social assistance from the state has always been the last resort (Leung & Nann, 1995; Wong, 1998). As later chapters in this book will show, many Dibao recipients still rely on relatives and friends for various forms of help.

Second, Chinese culture has always valued *education and work*, virtues also central to Confucianism. The expectation is that education will lead to stable, respectable jobs, and everyone should strive to work hard, be self-sufficient, and provide help and support to other members of the family and community when needed. This dominant social value makes it not only undesirable but also stigmatizing to apply for and receive social assistance. Throughout history, many Chinese citizens have chosen to go hungry and remain dignified rather than beg for support.

Third, in both Confucian tradition and the socialist regime, *the government assumes a paternalist role* in being responsible for providing social assistance to those in need. The public, in turn, expects the government to fulfill this role (Chen, 2012; Dixon, 1981). Built on the fundamental values concerning family, community, and work discussed earlier, the state is only expected to step in to provide a last-resort safety net when private sources fail to meet people's basic needs. Other less pressing needs, such as healthcare, education, and personal fulfillment, are traditionally beyond the responsibility of the state.

Lastly, *social harmony* has always been valued by the Taoist tradition in Chinese culture and more recently adopted by the Communist party as a central goal of its regime. Social assistance has functioned not only to support livelihood for the poor but as a means for political and social control. Both the ruling elite and the public share the view that social stability is essential for continued growth and prosperity of the country, and social assistance helps serve this larger purpose.

It is important to note that the four values and principles highlighted here are interlinked and bear inherent conundrums. For example, the value placed on family and community challenges the value of work and self-sufficiency, and the values of work, family, and community contradict that of state responsibility. The emphasis on social harmony versus work, self-sufficiency, family, and community points to the tension between individual and societal responsibilities and the dual functions of social assistance in supporting the poor and maintaining social control. Such conundrums exist in nearly all societies and remain the central themes of most policy debates in contemporary welfare systems (Ellwood, 1988).

THE GLOBAL CONTEXT: SOCIAL ASSISTANCE AROUND THE WORLD

Since the 1990s, there have been a growing number of both conditional and unconditional cash transfer programs in developing and developed countries that are aimed at reducing poverty and promoting human development (Barrientos, 2013). Unconditional cash transfer (UCT) programs like Dibao date back to at least the Roman Empire (Brown, 2002; Hands, 1968). By 2014, UCT programs had been implemented in 118 countries globally (Gentilini, Maddalena, & Ruslan, 2014). Eligibility for benefits is usually determined on the basis of means testing and sometimes family registration or formation. These programs have the advantages of having lower administrative cost and not constraining recipients' consumption choices. Recipients, therefore, can decide to use the transfer income where most needed, such as for housing or education, and respond to urgent needs such as healthcare.

Research has documented positive effects of such UCT programs on child cognitive achievement, health, educational attainment, income in adulthood, and longevity (Aizer, Eli, Ferrie, & Lleras-Muney, 2014; Dahl & Lochner, 2012; Milligan & Stabile, 2011). Some impact evaluation studies in developing countries have also observed a rise in families' consumption and improvement in children's human capital following participation in UCT programs (Baird, Ferreira, Özler, & Woolcock, 2014; Baird, McIntosh, & Özler, 2011; Barrientos & Dejong, 2006; Case & Deaton, 1998; Devereux, Marshall, MacAshkill, & Pelham, 2005; Duflo, 2003; Haushofer & Shapiro, 2016; Robertson et al., 2013).

In contrast, conditional cash transfer (CCT) programs make welfare receipt conditional on recipients' actions in human capital investment, such as school enrollment for children and regular doctor's visits. The scope of CCT programs has grown enormously during the past decade, especially in Latin America and the Caribbean but also in some developed countries and regions. The main rationale for this approach is that poor families not only have tight budget constraints but also tend to underestimate future returns on human capital investment because of their limited information and the lack of positive role models. This in turn leads to low spending on children's education and health and reinforces intergenerational transmission of poverty (Attanasio & Kaufmann, 2014; Das, Do, & Özler, 2005; de Janvry & Sadoulet, 2006; Dizon-Ross, 2014; Jensen, 2010). It is also evident that day-to-day hard choices associated with poverty distract poor people from long-term planning (e.g., children's education) and keep their aspirations at a low level (Bernard, Dercon, Orkin, & Taffesse, 2014; Chiapa, Garrido, & Prina, 2012; Mani, Mullainathan, Shafir, & Zhao, 2013; Mullainathan & Shafir, 2013). By making cash transfers conditional on human investment, CCT programs explicitly tackle these problems and guide low-income families to invest in human capital and enable their children to move out of poverty.

The effects of CCT programs have been rigorously evaluated in the literature, partly because their setup conveniently allows the use of randomized controlled trials (RCTs) for evaluation purposes and partly because of the focus on human development outcomes. A review of the evaluation of CCT programs across several countries has documented clear positive effects on increased school enrollment, improved preventive healthcare, and greater household consumption, particularly consumption of more nutritious foods (Attanasio & Mesnard, 2006; Barrientos, 2013; Fiszbein et al., 2009; Hoddinott & Skoufias, 2004). CCT programs have also shown positive effects on children's long-term outcomes in education and health (Baird et al., 2014; Ranganathan & Lagarde, 2012; Rawlings & Rubio, 2005).

In this broad context, Dibao is currently the world's largest UCT program in terms of population coverage. It is, however, unique in several regards. First, its means testing is very strict and involves extensive public participation and scrutiny, making it more stigmatizing than many other similar programs. This is partly because of China's lack of an established system that contain reliable information on employment and income, which could have spared participants some of the extensive, intrusive means testing procedures.

Second, Dibao is centrally regulated but locally implemented, along with the very diverse local economic development, fiscal capacity, and political and institutional dynamics in China. The dilemma between central control and local autonomy often leads to disparities in Dibao's performance and effectiveness across localities. It also breeds room for corruption and other misconducts of local officials.

Third, Dibao is an integral part of the rapidly evolving Chinese social benefit system that has been shifting from welfare socialism to welfare capitalism (Carrillo & Duckett, 2011; Gao, Yang, & Li, 2013; Leung & Xu, 2015). Its development thus reflects many other broader trends and issues that China is dealing with during this transition. These include taking over as the world's largest economy but with a slowing of economic growth, urbanization, aging of the population, and demands for equal rights, openness, and democracy (Duckett, 2012;

Frazier, 2014; Saich, 2008, 2015). As China moves toward building a stronger, unified social benefit system in response to these trends, it is important to monitor and evaluate Dibao's role and performance against the broader political and socioeconomic context.

SCOPE OF BOOK AND PREVIEW OF FINDINGS

It has been over 20 years since Dibao's inception, yet there has not been a systematic evaluation of its impact and effectiveness. This book fills this gap by synthesizing the vast yet scattered existing evidence (in both English and Chinese, both quantitative and qualitative), providing an updated, comprehensive evaluation of Dibao's performance, and offering timely and practical policy implications. Importantly, this book offers new analysis of the performance of rural Dibao, given its relatively short history and scarce existing evidence in the literature.

The book includes nine chapters. Chapter 2 traces the background, inception, and development of Dibao. Chapter 3 uses administrative data to describe the patterns in Dibao thresholds, financing, and beneficiaries and discusses its decentralized implementation. Chapters 4 through 8 focus on evaluation of Dibao's impact on various outcomes and its effectiveness. Specifically, Chapter 4 examines Dibao's targeting performance. Chapter 5 investigates Dibao's anti-poverty effectiveness. Chapter 6 reviews a series of welfare-to-work initiatives and evaluates their impact. Chapter 7 focuses on Dibao's influence on family expenditures. Chapter 8 investigates the association between receiving Dibao and recipients' social participation as well as subjective well-being. Lastly, Chapter 9 discusses policy solutions and research directions for the future.

As a preview of the findings, Chapter 2 shows that, throughout its development, Dibao has been shaped by economic and political forces and remained true to its dual functions of serving as a safety net for the poor and maintaining social control and political stability. With Dibao, there has been constant wrestling with the fundamental question of how to conduct means testing and determine eligibility most effectively and achieve its intended goal of serving as a safety net for the truly poor. Such challenges are embedded in the dilemma between central regulation and local implementation of Dibao and will continue in its future development.

Chapter 3 shows that both urban and rural Dibao have undergone significant expansion in their thresholds, benefit levels, expenditures, population coverage, and number of beneficiaries over the years, with the expansions being more rapid and dramatic in rural than in urban areas. However, the Dibao assistance standards remain low relative to average consumption levels, manifesting Dibao's fundamental role as a last-resort, bare-minimum safety net program. Despite its decentralized implementation and the requirement that local governments establish a budget, Dibao expenditures have been heavily subsidized by the central government. Dibao's population coverage in both urban and rural areas increased rapidly during the early stages of implementation but has leveled off and even declined in recent years.

Chapter 4 documents the existence of substantial targeting errors in both urban and rural Dibao. With regard to population targeting, across urban and rural areas, significant numbers of eligible families were mistakenly excluded (or "leaked") from receiving Dibao benefits, while others were mis-targeted or included erroneously in Dibao coverage. Rural Dibao had more severe exclusion and mis-targeting errors than urban Dibao. Urban Dibao benefits were concentrated more among the poor than were the rural benefits. Both urban and rural areas had significant benefit gaps as reflected by the large differences between the amount families were entitled to receive and the actual amount received. Despite these errors and gaps, however, Dibao's targeting performance is actually better than many other similar programs around the world.

Chapter 5 shows that, based on various poverty thresholds (also known as "poverty lines") across urban and rural areas, Dibao's anti-poverty effectiveness is limited and at best modest, largely due to its targeting errors and gaps in benefit delivery. Dibao is more effective at reducing the depth and severity of poverty than the poverty rate, and its anti-poverty effectiveness is greater among recipients than in the general population. Dibao's influence on reducing poverty is greater when a lower poverty threshold is used and smaller when a higher poverty threshold is used. Because relative poverty lines are often set as a percentage of the median income in the society and tend to be much higher than the more widely used absolute poverty lines, Dibao's effects on reducing relative poverty are particularly limited. Dibao had minimal effects on narrowing the income inequality gap in society.

Chapter 6 discusses various barriers for Dibao recipients to move from welfare to work, leading many to be unwillingly labeled "welfare dependents." These barriers include limited employability due to poor health, low education, lack of skills, middle age, long history of unemployment, lack of financial or social capital, family care responsibilities, lack of child and senior care services in the community, stigma from neighbors and local officials, and a series of policy design factors that deter work efforts. Local governments have experimented with an array of welfare-to-work programs, ranging from punitive approaches to protective measures, to those offering direct incentive for seeking and maintaining jobs and providing job trainings and referrals. These initiatives, however, have not been systematically evaluated. The limited existing evidence shows that they are ineffective in helping Dibao recipients move from welfare to work.

Chapter 7 documents the high expenditure required for healthcare and education that is faced by most urban and rural Dibao families, especially those with children or members who have severe or chronic disease. While Dibao benefits have enabled urban recipient families to spend more on both of these items, it has helped rural families pay for healthcare but not education. Meeting survival needs is not found to be a priority in the use of Dibao benefits for either urban or rural recipients, which suggests that these families may be maintaining a bare minimum level of livelihood while having to meet urgent health or education needs. In both urban and rural areas, receiving Dibao is associated with reduced spending on leisure. Rural Dibao recipients spend less on alcohol, tobacco, gifts to others, and social insurance contributions; the same effect is either not found or has not been examined in urban Dibao.

Chapter 8 discusses some unintended associations between Dibao and behavioral and subjective outcomes among both urban and rural recipients. Dibao recipients tend to live a more isolated and detached life and engage in fewer leisure and social activities than their non-recipient peers. The stigma, shame, and despair associated with receiving Dibao and the poor outlook for improved income and social class may lead recipients to be unhappy and feel dissatisfied with their lives. There is also some evidence that receiving Dibao is associated with less time spent on education and work activities, echoing the many challenges faced by Dibao recipients in moving from welfare to work.

Based on the extensive evidence presented in earlier chapters and drawing from the international literature, Chapter 9 proposes several policy solutions for improving Dibao's performance and suggests future research directions that can help further the monitoring and evaluation of Dibao. With regard to Dibao's policy design, improvements can be made to set higher assistance standards, raise benefit levels, broaden its population coverage, and revise its stigmatizing means-testing procedures. Dibao's implementation can be improved by offering more public education about Dibao, building a more professional team of Dibao administrators, and having greater involvement of and collaboration with the non-governmental sector. Dibao's performance can also be improved through better coordination with other social welfare programs and better fit within the rapidly expanding, broader social benefit system. The monitoring and evaluation of Dibao can benefit from more rigorous, better coordinated, longitudinal research studies examining multidimensional outcomes and joint efforts by interdisciplinary scholars, government officials, and international organizations.

2
BACKGROUND, INCEPTION, AND DEVELOPMENT

Dibao was initiated in Shanghai in 1993 and implemented nationwide in urban areas in 1999 and in rural areas in 2007. Between and since these milestones, Dibao has undergone significant expansions and impacted the lives of millions of low-income families. It is not only China's flagship social assistance program but currently the world's largest such program in terms of population coverage. Against what economic and political background was Dibao established? How has it been regulated and how has it grown over the years? This chapter traces Dibao's background and evolvement, documents its development over the years, and discusses the implications of these developments.

BACKGROUND AND INCEPTION

Since the mid-to-late 1980s, a series of economic and social policy reforms have created a new group of urban poor in China. On the one hand, during the market reform process, many state-owned and collective enterprises went bankrupt, and others had massive layoffs in an attempt to improve economic productivity and efficiency, yielding a sharply rising unemployment rate in urban China. The official urban unemployment rate rose from 2.0% in 1988 to 3.1% in 2000 and kept increasing to 4.2% in 2004. The number of laid-off workers from state-owned enterprises (SOEs) was 5.9 million in 1998 and peaked at 6.6 million in 2000 (National Bureau of Statistics [NBS], 2005a). Still, these figures are underestimates. They leave out the many who are not officially laid off but stay on the job roster and receive very low or no earnings. Those who have no jobs but are not officially registered as unemployed are also excluded (Feng, Hu, & Moffitt, 2015).

On the other hand, a series of social policy changes in urban areas have focused on shifting the welfare payment responsibility from employers to be shared by employers and employees, to facilitate market-oriented economic reforms. The state-owned and collective enterprises, which were the major providers of social benefits, needed to lower costs and improve productivity. Consequently, urban social benefits have been transformed from their original broad coverage and generous provision to playing a much smaller role in the lives of families (Gao, 2006; Hussain, 2007). The financing of most social benefits has shifted from work units to general taxes or shared responsibilities among individuals, employers, and, sometimes, the government. More social benefit programs such as pension and healthcare required direct individual contributions. Empirical evidence shows that, on average, social benefits comprised one quarter of urban families' total household income in 2002, shrinking significantly from 44% in 1988 (Gao & Riskin, 2009).

These economic and social policy reforms left many who previously enjoyed both secure employment and comprehensive and generous social benefits without a job or social protection. The growing number of the "new urban poor" became an increasing threat to social stability, providing direct political incentive for both local and central governments to reinstate the government's paternalist role and establish a last resort for the poor.

Against this backdrop and enabled by its strong fiscal capacity and relative political autonomy to set local policies, in 1993, Shanghai was the first to establish its urban Dibao program. The city government organized a series of meetings to discuss how to support the basic livelihood of various low-income groups, including low-wage earners, the unemployed, retirees, and others with no stable income source. One key charge of the meetings was that any new policy or program to solve this problem had to ensure both continued economic development and social stability. Based on surveys and fieldwork, on June 1, 1993, Shanghai established its urban Dibao program.

The initial Dibao assistance standard (or "Dibao line" or "threshold") in Shanghai was set at 120 monthly yuan per capita. This standard was developed on the basis of an assessment of the local sustenance level. To maintain its intended nature as a bare-minimum, last-resort safety net, it was also set to be lower than the local minimum wage, living subsidy to laid-off workers, and unemployment insurance benefit. In that first year, a total of 7,680 individuals were beneficiaries of the Shanghai urban Dibao (Hong, 2005a; Liu, 2010).

As is evident in Dibao's background and inception in Shanghai, both economic and political driving forces are key to the establishment of Dibao. In fact, the two fundamental goals of Dibao—to provide a safety net for the poor and to maintain social and political stability—directly reflect these twin driving forces. China's transition from a planned to market economy was the most influential factor in the establishment of the Dibao program. As inherent in any capitalist economy, market competitions left some people behind and created the "new poor" in China. This group includes those suffering from poor health, disability, old age, and unemployment. Meanwhile, China's economic reforms focused on layoffs and lifting the previously heavy social benefit burdens from state and collective employers so as to stimulate economic growth and efficiency. Dibao served as a powerful tool of social control to prevent public protests from this disadvantaged group formerly enjoying job security and social benefits but now left behind and vulnerable. Throughout its development and expansions in both urban and rural areas, as detailed next, Dibao has remained true to its dual functions of serving as a last-resort safety net and maintaining social control.

DEVELOPMENT STAGES AND REGULATIONS

From Dibao's inception in Shanghai in 1993, its development can be divided into four stages, each with important milestones and regulations, as outlined in Table 2.1. The first stage was from 1993 to 1999, during which Dibao moved from local experiments to nationwide establishment in urban areas.

Stage 1: From Local Experiments to Nationwide Establishment of Urban Dibao (1993–1999)

Encouraged by Shanghai's successful example and facing similar challenges, several other cities soon experimented with their own Dibao programs. By January 1995, five other cities—Xiamen, Qingdao, Fuzhou, Dalian, and Shenyang—established their Dibao programs. These early successes garnered lots of public support and increasing attention from the Ministry of Civil Affairs (MCA) in the central government. In May 1995, the MCA organized two important meetings—one in Qingdao and the other in Xiamen, both cities that had established Dibao by then—attended by selected provincial and city officials who were in charge of social assistance. These meetings summarized the experiences and lessons learned from the early cities and prepared for the launching of urban Dibao nationwide (Hong, 2005b).

Specifically, the meetings emphasized several key points based on the experiences of the early cities implementing Dibao. First, Dibao eligibility needed to be determined on the basis of applicants' income level instead of age, working ability, or employment status. Employed and unemployed persons as well as retirees could all be recipients as long as they met the eligibility requirements. Second, Dibao assistance standards needed to be set using scientific approaches to ensure the basic livelihood of the poor population. These standards also needed to be adjusted annually according to the local economic development level, consumption standard, and consumer price indices (CPIs). Third, financing for Dibao had to be guaranteed through shared responsibility among different levels of government and supplemented by the central government when necessary. Fourth, Dibao needed to be implemented by local governments through strict screening and approval procedures and monitored by the public and the media. Lastly,

Table 2.1. Stages and Milestones of Dibao Development

Stage, Year, and Regulation-issuing Entity	Milestone/Major Regulation	Main Content of Regulation
Stage 1: From Local Experiments to Nationwide Establishment of Urban Dibao (1993–1999)		
June 1993, Shanghai city government	Shanghai established its Dibao program on June 1, 1993.	
January 1995, selected city governments	By January 1995, Xiamen, Qingdao, Fuzhou, Dalian, and Shenyang had established their Dibao programs.	
1996, MCA	Opinion on Accelerating the Establishment of the Rural Social Welfare System	Pushed for more local experiments with rural Dibao and suggested establishment of rural Dibao as an integral part of the rural social welfare system
September 1997, State Council	Announcement on the Establishment of the Urban Dibao Program Nationwide	Stipulated that all cities should implement Dibao by the end of 1999
September 1999, State Council	Regulations on the Urban Dibao Program	Formally established urban Dibao nationwide and provided regulations on the assistance standard, target population, implementation, and financing of urban Dibao
Stage 2: Expansions in Urban Dibao and Nationwide Establishment of Rural Dibao (2000–2007)		
2001, State Council	Notification about Further Strengthening the Urban Dibao Program	Required full coverage of all eligible people and full delivery of benefits (yingbao jinbao)
April 2003, MCA	Notification about Strengthening Social Assistance to Rural Families with Extreme Hardships	Required provision of regular social assistance in cash or in kind to rural families who did not qualify for Wubao assistance but faced extreme hardship because of having no family support, disability, or severe illness

(continued)

Table 2.1. Continued

Stage, Year, and Regulation-issuing Entity	Milestone/Major Regulation	Main Content of Regulation
July 2007, State Council	Notification about Establishing the Rural Dibao Program Nationwide	Formally established rural Dibao nationwide and offered regulations on the assistance standard, target population, implementation, and financing of the rural Dibao

Stage 3: Stabilization and Standardization of Urban and Rural Dibao (2007–2013)

October 2008, MCA	Regulations on Identifying Low-Income Families in the Cities	Aimed at greater accuracy in means testing, establishing a relatively complete information system on family economic conditions, and broadening coverage of supplementary social assistance programs to all low-income families
June 2010, MCA	Notification about Further Strengthening the Targeting Performance of the Urban Dibao	Specified a set of rules to be applied to identifying Dibao's eligible population accurately
May 2011, MCA	Instructions for Further Regulating the Establishment and Adjustment of Urban and Rural Dibao Lines	Addressed the lack of standardization across localities in criteria and procedures used for setting and adjusting Dibao assistance standards
September 2012, State Council	Opinion about Further Strengthening and Enhancing Dibao Implementation	Outlined guiding principles and concrete measures to improve various aspects of Dibao implementation in both urban and rural areas

Stage 4: Toward the Establishment of a Comprehensive Social Assistance System (since 2014)

February 2014, State Council	Provisional Regulations on Social Assistance	Important step toward establishment of a comprehensive social assistance system through the law. The system contains Dibao and a series of other social assistance programs.

Dibao beneficiaries with additional needs could receive additional support for education and housing (Hong, 2005b).

With the strong endorsement and support of the MCA, by August 1997, a total of 206 cities—one third of all Chinese cities—had established their Dibao programs. In September 1997, the State Council issued the "Announcement on the Establishment of the Urban Dibao Program Nationwide" and stipulated that all cities should implement Dibao by the end of 1999. On September 28, 1999, the State Council issued the "Regulations on the Urban Dibao Program" that launched the national urban Dibao and guided its implementation. By October 1999, all 668 cities and 1,689 counties in urban China had implemented the Dibao program (Liu, 2010; State Council Information Office [SCIO], 2004).

Meanwhile, several provinces experimented with rural Dibao during the 1990s, but the early development of rural Dibao was unbalanced across regions and did not gain national traction until after 2005. In 1994, Shanxi was the first province to experiment with rural Dibao. In 1996, the MCA issued the "Opinion on Accelerating the Establishment of the Rural Social Welfare System" that pushed for more local experiments with rural Dibao. This opinion also suggested the establishment of rural Dibao as an integral part of the rural social welfare system, even if the assistance standards needed to be set at low levels initially.

Similar to the early developments in urban Dibao, rural Dibao was first adopted much more in the eastern region and rural areas surrounding big cities, despite some experiments in selected localities in the central and western regions and poor counties. These early explorations with rural Dibao remained unbalanced, with wealthier cities and provinces, such as Shanghai, Zhejiang, Fujian, and Jiangsu, establishing higher assistance standards and broader population coverage while localities in central and western regions lacked fiscal capacity to support this program (Zhang & Xu, 2006).

Stage 2: Expansions in Urban Dibao and Nationwide Establishment of Rural Dibao (2000–2007)

The second stage in Dibao development was from 2000 to 2007, during which urban Dibao was much expanded and rural Dibao was further developed and achieved nationwide establishment in 2007. For urban Dibao, in 2001, just 2 years after its national implementation, the State Council issued the "Notification about Further Strengthening the Urban Dibao Program" to require full coverage of all eligible people and full delivery of Dibao benefits (*yingbao jinbao*). This led to gradual yet steady increases in the average urban Dibao threshold as well as the total urban Dibao expenditures during 2001–2007. A more direct response to this notification was the sharp increase in the total number of urban Dibao recipients from 2001 to 2002 in absolute terms and as a percentage of the urban population. Both the absolute number of urban Dibao recipients and its share in the urban population jumped by about

75% from 2001 to 2002, which then slowed down and leveled off during the remaining years of this stage.

Influenced by the success of the urban Dibao but facing the challenges of unbalanced development and fiscal capacity, rural Dibao adopted an incremental approach to provide social assistance to families in need. In April 2003, the MCA issued the "Notification about Strengthening Social Assistance to Rural Families with Extreme Hardships." This notification stated that social assistance in rural China should follow the principles of "government providing assistance, societal mutual help, elder support by adult children, and stabilizing farmland policies" as outlined by the State Council (Liu, 2010, p. 23). It required localities to provide regular social assistance in cash or in kind to rural families who did not qualify for Wubao assistance but faced extreme hardships due to lack of family support or having disability or severe illness. Most localities that did not have the rural Dibao in place soon set up this hardship assistance program, but its coverage and assistance level were very limited, especially in poor localities (Zhang & Xu, 2006).

To address this unbalanced situation and provide social assistance to all rural families in need, in July 2007, the State Council issued the "Notification about Establishing the Rural Dibao Program Nationwide." This notification required the formal establishment of the rural Dibao program nationwide by the end of the year and offered regulations on the assistance standard, target population, implementation, and financing of the rural Dibao. The central government committed 3 billion yuan to support localities that had financial difficulties and ensure the successful nationwide implementation of the rural Dibao. By the end of September 2007, all 2,777 counties that covered rural areas had established the rural Dibao.

Stage 3: Stabilization and Standardization of Urban and Rural Dibao (2007–2013)

The third stage of Dibao development was from 2007 to 2013, during which both urban and rural Dibao was stabilized, and a series of regulations issued by the central government focused on the standardization of Dibao implementation across localities. For urban Dibao, a series of regulations issued during this period focused on improving Dibao's targeting performance and assistance standards to achieve enhanced implementation. Urban Dibao development in this stage is characterized by stable annual increases in the Dibao assistance standards but constant decreases in its population coverage after 2010. Rural Dibao development during this stage expanded continually, as reflected by the constantly rising Dibao assistance standards and growing population coverage throughout this period.

From 2008 to 2011, a series of regulations focused on improving Dibao's targeting performance and assistance standards. In October 2008, the MCA issued the "Regulations on Identifying Low-Income Families in the Cities." The regulations clarified that both income and assets would be considered according to local standards when determining whether a family could be identified as a low-income family. According to these regulations, being able to identify low-income families accurately served as the foundation for implementing Dibao and extending coverage of supplementary social assistance programs, such as housing, medical, education, and temporary assistance; it was also a crucial step in establishing a comprehensive urban social assistance system. These regulations aimed at being more accurate in means testing, establishing a relatively complete information system on family economic conditions, and ultimately broadening the coverage of the supplementary social assistance programs to all low-income families.

In June 2010, the MCA issued the "Notification about Further Strengthening the Targeting Performance of the Urban Dibao" to specify a set of rules to be applied to identifying Dibao's eligible population accurately. This notification was triggered by the leakage and mis-targeting issues disclosed in various localities and was aimed at addressing these issues with specific measures. With regard to Dibao eligibility rules, the notification restated that only those with local urban household registration status (or Hukou) were eligible for Dibao benefits; rural Hukou holders with extreme hardships needed to provide proof that they were not receiving rural Dibao before being considered for urban Dibao. The notification further specified that all sources of family income and assets, such as savings, stocks, owned housing, and vehicles, needed to be considered in means testing. It also emphasized that the incomes of all family members in the household had to be counted, including income from wages, businesses, property, and transfers.

This notification specified a set of rules with regard to means testing procedures:

(1) Street (jiedao)- or township-level government offices instead of the community level should be in charge of Dibao application screening and approval.

(2) Household visits and interviews for the purpose of means testing should be conducted by a team of at least two members and all original information collected during this process should be kept on file.

(3) Participatory appraisal of Dibao eligibility should be done among a group of at least seven members, such as community resident committee members, street or community Dibao workers, and community resident representatives, on a rotating basis.

(4) Public display of the names of potential Dibao recipients should be done within the community in such a way that the privacy of families, especially children, was protected.

(5) Departments of civil affairs at the county level should randomly select at least 20% of all Dibao families to double check family income and Dibao eligibility to ensure accuracy.

The notification reiterated the push for establishing a comprehensive urban social assistance system that would contain information about urban families' income sources and social benefit receipt as proposed in the 2008 regulations.

In May 2011, the MCA issued the "Instructions for Further Regulating the Establishment and Adjustment of Urban and Rural Dibao Assistance Standards" to address the lack of standardization across localities in the criteria and procedures used for setting and adjusting the Dibao thresholds. This set of instructions prescribed three methods to be used in setting and adjusting the Dibao thresholds: (1) according to the level of local basic living expenses, (2) on the basis of the local Engel coefficient, and (3) relative to local average consumption level. The use of these methods was to be carried out through coordinated efforts across various government departments and following standardized procedures.

Specifically, using the first method, the Dibao threshold, or Dibao line, is set as equivalent to the level of local basic living expenses on necessary food and non-food items. Among these, food expenses are estimated according to the necessary energy intake level and their corresponding food items as recommended and published by the Chinese Nutrition Society. Non-food expenses need to be sufficient to maintain basic livelihood and include items such as clothing, water, electricity, gas, transportation, and other necessities. These expenses are to be estimated on the basis of market prices or survey data and can be adjusted according to local income or consumption level as well as local economic development and fiscal capacity.

Using the second method, the Dibao line is calculated as the necessary food expenses divided by the local Engel coefficient for the lowest income group during the past year. The Engel coefficient measures the percentage of household income used for food purchases. This method aims to ensure that the Dibao line reflects the total household consumption level of the poorest group and captures both food and non-food expenses. Similar to the first method, the estimated Dibao line can be adjusted on the basis of local income and consumption levels as well as economic development and fiscal capacity.

The third method builds on the first and second methods and further uses the local average consumption level as a benchmark for setting and adjusting the Dibao line. Specifically, once the local Dibao line is estimated using one of the first two methods, its percentage in the local average consumption level for the past year is calculated. Then, this percentage can be applied directly to the annual average consumption levels for the next few years to achieve the annually adjusted Dibao line. Compared to the first two methods, this method is less costly and more widely adopted, as it does not require annual estimations of food and non-food expenses (Umapathi, Wang, & O'Keefe, 2013). It also helps to ensure that the Dibao line keeps pace with the local average consumption level.

In sum, the series of regulations issued during 2008–2011 aimed at improving Dibao's targeting performance and standardizing the methods and procedures used for assessing Dibao eligibility and setting Dibao assistance standards. It showcased the MCA's determination to address Dibao's targeting errors and regulate the varied local implementations. It also highlighted that Dibao development might be moving into a new era of tighter regulations from the central government and becoming a more integral part of the national social benefit system.

In September 2012, the State Council issued the "Opinion about Further Strengthening and Enhancing Dibao Implementation," which outlined the guiding principles and concrete measures to improve various aspects of Dibao implementation in both urban and rural areas. The four guiding principles included full coverage and delivery of benefits; transparency, equity, and fairness; dynamic management to ensure timely assessment of Dibao eligibility and benefit levels; and a coordinated and balanced approach that takes into consideration urban–rural and regional differences and developmental stages of localities and connects Dibao with other social benefit programs.

Building on and drawing from the 2008–2011 series of regulations, this opinion further specified a set of concrete measures to be followed in Dibao implementation. First, it reiterated that Dibao eligibility should be determined on the basis of applicants' local Hukou status, household income, and assets. Local Dibao lines need to be set using one of the three methods prescribed in the 2011 instructions and adjusted annually. Second, Dibao's screening and approval process should include the following steps: application, screening through in-home visits, participatory appraisal, approval (with at least 30% potential recipients subject to double checking through random selection), public display and feedback, and timely delivery of benefits. All of these steps were aimed at standardizing Dibao's implementation procedures and minimizing its targeting errors.

Third, this opinion pushed for the establishment of a family income information sharing and verification system that is coordinated among various government departments horizontally and across various levels of government vertically. It emphasized that a dynamic management approach be adopted so that Dibao eligibility and benefit levels could be monitored and assessed in a timely manner and welfare dependency among the beneficiaries could be reduced. The opinion specified that the verification of Dibao eligibility and benefit levels for Sanwu individuals (those without working ability, income source, or family support) be done annually; for families with no significant income changes in the short run, this verification could be done biannually; and for families with irregular income sources and whose members have working capacity, the verification should be done monthly in the cities and quarterly in rural areas.

Lastly, this opinion emphasized the importance of monitoring, auditing, and public reporting of corruption, embezzlement, mis-targeting, and other misconduct in Dibao implementation and pushed for the establishment and strengthening of such infrastructure within and across relevant government departments. It also reiterated the need to connect Dibao with its supplementary social assistance programs, such as housing, medical, education, and temporary assistance, as well as social insurance programs, such as pensions and medical insurance. Urban Dibao needed to be connected more closely with work support programs to enable welfare-to-work transitions while rural Dibao needed to be better connected with other anti-poverty policies and programs.

All in all, this stage saw significant expansions in Dibao development, especially in rural areas. Meanwhile, the central government moved to have tighter control over Dibao's implementation, with a focus on improving its targeting performance; standardizing its assistance levels and screening, verification, and approval procedures; and establishing effective systems for information sharing, management monitoring, and coordination among various social assistance and insurance programs.

Stage 4: Toward the Establishment of a Comprehensive Social Assistance System (since 2014)

The last stage of Dibao development, the period since 2014 when the State Council issued the "Provisional Regulations on Social Assistance," is an important step toward the establishment of a comprehensive social assistance system through the law (SCIO, 2014). This set of regulations stated that social assistance is meant to provide a last resort and offer support in urgent situations and hardships. It should be sustainable and connected with other policies and programs within the broad social benefit system. The level of social assistance should keep pace with the level of socioeconomic development.

Most importantly, this set of regulations clearly listed all of the main social assistance programs and outlined their respective guiding principles and procedures. Dibao was listed as the predominant social assistance program supplemented by a series of other programs, including support and care for those with extreme hardship; assistance to natural disaster victims; and medical, education, housing, employment, and temporary assistance. The regulations encouraged the participation and support of organizations and individuals through charitable donations, partnering with programs, providing professional services, and offering voluntary services. In particular, the regulations urged a more active role of social service agencies and professional social workers in helping to promote social inclusion, empowerment, and subjective well-being of social assistance recipients and connect them with available resources. These regulations emphasized the importance of management monitoring and law enforcement in following these principles and implementing these procedures.

The specific regulations on Dibao mostly reiterated what was outlined in the 2012 opinion issued by the State Council. This set of regulations, however, notably omited the earlier requirement of local Hukou as a Dibao eligibility criterion. In the news conference announcing the issuing of these regulations, Minister Li Liguo of the MCA clarified that all of the social assistance programs included in the regulations were set in the national instead of the urban–rural dual contexts. Governmental departments above the county level were responsible for setting and adjusting the assistance standards, screening and approval procedures, financial resources, management monitoring, and law enforcement. In particular, Minister Li stated that the temporary assistance program should cover urban residents who have no local Hukou but have lived in cities for a certain period of time. Further, for selected social assistance programs with relatively consistent assistance standards such as medical assistance, the same standard and benefit level should apply to both urban and rural beneficiaries (SCIO, 2014).

Importantly, with regard to both Dibao and support to individuals with extreme hardship, Minister Li stated that the assistance standards should be established following scientific, quantitative methods so that they are more balanced and less differentiated across the urban–rural areas. Local governments with greater urban–rural homogeneity and financial capacities are encouraged to narrow the gaps in assistance standards gradually and achieve consistency across the urban–rural areas. Minister Li also noted, however, that it would require a process to remove the urban–rural differences entirely given the different income sources, assets, work and business conditions, and consumption levels across the two areas. These regulations and their interpretations, nonetheless, point to a new direction toward gradually narrowing and eliminating the urban–rural differences that have dominated Dibao's development (SCIO, 2014).

This new policy direction has led to some early progress toward the narrowing of the urban–rural Dibao gaps. Solinger (2015b) documented that, by July 2015, several major cities, including Beijing, Shanghai, Nanjing, Hangzhou, Changsha, Chengdu, and Hefei, had raised their urban and rural Dibao assistance standards to an equal level, while some others were still considering making such a transition and carrying out experiments or setting up trial districts.

Despite its short duration, this last stage formally established Dibao as a central and integral part of China's expanding social assistance system. Through listing and specifying the various social assistance programs within this system, Dibao and other programs can be more focused on their respective intended goals and functions in their implementations. Accordingly, their performance and effectiveness can be better evaluated and improved. Given the short duration and lack of implementation evidence thus far, the long-term impact and consequences of this stage are yet to be monitored and assessed.

SUMMARY AND IMPLICATIONS

This chapter traces Dibao's background, inception, and development stages and documents its milestones and significant regulations. Throughout its establishment and development, Dibao has been shaped by economic and political forces and remained true to its dual functions of serving as a safety net to the poor and maintaining social control and political stability. Urban Dibao was developed before rural Dibao because urban economic reforms dissolved the former "full employment" system as well as its embedded comprehensive and generous social benefits and thus brought about more immediate threats to social stability in the urban areas. Rural Dibao became the focus only after urban Dibao had been significantly expanded and the unbalanced treatment of the urban and rural poor became a threat to social stability and cohesion. The continued economic growth, coupled with strong political rule of the government during this period, helped ensure Dibao's development and expansion.

As is the case for similar means-tested programs around the world, it is evident that Dibao has to wrestle with the fundamental question of how to conduct means testing and determine eligibility most effectively and achieve its intended goal of serving as a safety net for the truly poor. Throughout its various development stages, multiple regulations have specified Dibao eligibility rules, screening procedures, and monitoring mechanisms in an effort to improve its targeting performance. Yet these efforts, as well as the huge variations in their decentralized implementation, highlight the continued challenge in achieving this goal. Global evidence suggests that means testing is costly and often not very effective, especially in developing countries where information sharing systems and coordinated infrastructure are lacking (Barrientos, 2013; World Bank, 2015). Moving forward, this remains a fundamental challenge in Dibao's implementation and achievement of its full coverage and delivery goals, despite the recent regulations specifying the detailed rules and procedures for means testing.

The recent developments in Dibao, especially the issuing of the 2014 regulations, suggest both promising and concerning messages. On the promising side, there is a clear shift toward elimination of the urban–rural gap and a more balanced approach in serving urban and rural residents as well as the rural-to-urban migrant population. It is also very encouraging that the government is working to establish a comprehensive social assistance program centering around Dibao, but with separate programs to address specific needs of disadvantaged populations. These new movements, if actively pursued and sustained, would enhance social protection for the poor and those in need and help achieve greater equity and economic justice among the Chinese population.

On the concerning side, the specific regulations on eligibility rules and screening procedures and the standardization of Dibao lines that intend to address imbalances and misconduct across localities could be too rigid and backfire. For example, the rules for verification and close monitoring of Dibao eligibility and benefit levels may scare people away and deter some families truly in need from applying for benefits, as is evident in welfare programs in the United States (Edin & Shaefer, 2015). It may also push some families off the welfare roll when they gain some irregular income in the short run but fall back to poverty soon thereafter. In reality, it is often difficult or at least takes a long time for these families to reclaim their Dibao eligibility. As a consequence, such measures may actually deter work efforts, as these families may be afraid of losing their Dibao eligibility due to additional earned income, however temporary that income may be (Solinger, 2009). The standardization of Dibao lines could also lead to local resistance and incapacity, which in turn might diminish Dibao's coverage and effectiveness.

All of these issues are inherent challenges for Dibao and other means-tested social assistance programs around the world, with no simple solutions. Most of the remaining chapters in this book examine how Dibao has influenced certain aspects of outcomes for beneficiaries, offering policy implications based on empirical evidence. Continued research efforts are needed to monitor Dibao's new developments and their effectiveness to provide timely feedback and solutions for its future direction.

3

THRESHOLDS, FINANCING, AND BENEFICIARIES

As is evident from Chapter 2, local governments have considerable lati-
tude in setting their own Dibao thresholds and carrying out means testing to determine who can be beneficiaries and how much in benefits they can
receive. These local autonomies, however, are subject to central regulations as
well as local financial capacities. This chapter uses administrative data to track
changes in Dibao thresholds, benefit levels, financing, population coverage,
and beneficiary characteristics over time and to contrast these trends across
urban and rural areas. It further demonstrates Dibao's decentralized implementation in China's broader political context and discusses its implications.
This set of macro-level evidence shows that, despite the significant expansions
in both urban and rural areas over the years, Dibao has remained true to its
core dual functions as both a minimum-level safety net and a political tool for
social control.

DIBAO THRESHOLDS

As stipulated by the multiple regulations issued by the central government, local
governments are responsible for setting up Dibao assistance standards (also
called Dibao lines or thresholds) that reflect the local minimum level of livelihood. This assistance standard, or line, is set as a monthly amount in yuan at the
per capita level. According to the 1999 regulations, the Dibao line should cover
basic food, clothing, and shelter needs, taking into consideration utility, medical
care, and tuition expenses (Hong, 2005a). In reality, however, the determination
of the Dibao lines is often restricted by local governments' fiscal capacity. Gao
and Riskin (2013) examined the Dibao lines in 35 large cities and found that
they were strongly positively correlated with city per capita income level, with

an estimated correlation coefficient of 0.87 in 2002 and 0.88 in 2005. Because of the assistance standard's minimum nature, local Dibao lines are often purpose-fully set to be lower than the local minimum wage and unemployment subsidies (Du & Park, 2007; Guan, 2005).

Since their national implementation, both the urban and rural Dibao thresh-olds have increased continually, thanks to the annual adjustments in an effort to reflect price changes. However, both urban and rural lines remained low relative to the average consumption level within the respective urban and rural areas, manifesting Dibao's bare minimum nature amidst the rapid economic growth in China during the past 20 years.

Figure 3.1 shows that both urban and rural average Dibao lines increased substantially over the years, but the pace of increase lagged behind that of the respective urban and rural consumer price indices (CPIs). The urban lines remained significantly higher than the rural ones, without or with adjusting for CPIs. However, the rural Dibao lines had a much higher annual growth rate than that of the urban ones, suggesting that the rural lines have been approaching the levels of the urban lines.

Specifically, the average urban Dibao line increased from 149 monthly yuan at the time of its national implementation in 1999 to 411 monthly yuan in 2014, with an annual growth rate of 7%. However, after adjusting for the urban CPIs, the average urban Dibao line increased from 168 monthly yuan in 1999 (in 2007 constant value) to 336 monthly yuan in 2014, with an annual growth rate of 5%, two percentage points lower than without CPIs adjustment. During the 2007–2014 period, the annual growth rate of the average urban Dibao line was 12% without adjusting for the CPIs and 8% after adjusting for the CPIs. These trends suggest that the real increase in the average urban Dibao line was slower than the increases in the consumer prices during this period.

At its inception, the average rural Dibao line was much lower than the urban line and has remained significantly lower since, mainly due to the lower living standards in rural areas. However, since its national implementation in 2007, the average rural Dibao line has increased much faster as compared to the urban line. Rising from 70 monthly yuan in 2007, the average rural Dibao line reached 231 monthly yuan in 2014, with an annual growth rate of 19% during those 7 years. After adjusting for the rural CPIs, the increase was somewhat slower, aver-aging an annual growth rate of 15% and reaching 185 monthly yuan in 2014 (in 2007 constant value). Still, the increase in the average rural Dibao line has out-paced that of the average urban Dibao line.

How did the Dibao lines compare against the average consumption levels? Figure 3.2 presents the trend in urban and rural average Dibao lines as a per-centage of the respective per capita consumption levels. Since 1999, the aver-age urban Dibao line as a percentage of per capita consumption first declined, then fluctuated, and then rose again. It accounted for 28% of the average urban consumption level in 1999 but dropped to only 20% by 2013, reflecting both the

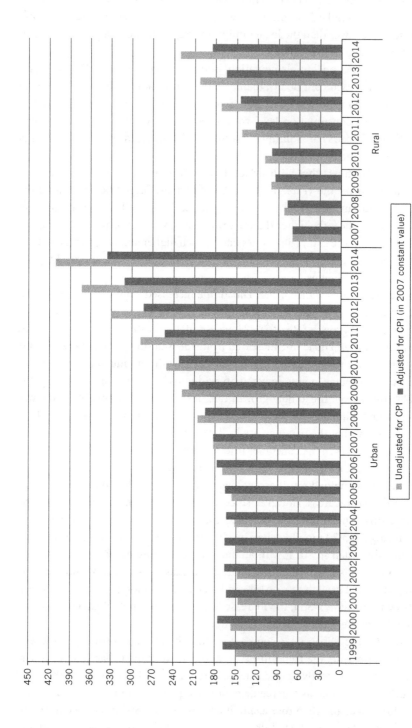

Figure 3.1. Trends in average urban and rural Dibao lines (monthly yuan). Sources: Figures unadjusted for consumer price indices (CPIs) are from Ministry of Civil Affairs (1999–2014); figures adjusted for CPIs are from author's calculations using unadjusted figures and official urban and rural CPIs, respectively.

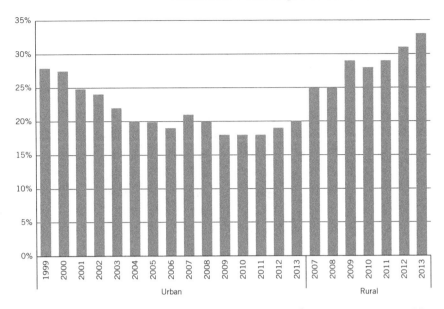

Figure 3.2. Urban and rural average Dibao lines as a percentage of per capita consumption (%). Sources: Author's calculations from Ministry of Civil Affairs (1999–2013) and National Bureau of Statistics (1999–2013b).

rising living standards in urban China during this period and the ebbing of the urban Dibao line relative to average consumption level.

The seemingly lower rural Dibao line in Figure 3.1 turns out to be higher than the urban line when measured as a percentage of the average consumption level. It kept increasing from 25% of the average rural consumption level in 2007 to 33% in 2013, despite a small drop in 2010, indicating that the lower nominal amounts of rural benefits may enable rural recipients to achieve a higher relative consumption level than that of their urban peers. It is important to note, however, that both the urban and rural average Dibao lines remained low relative to average consumption levels and stayed true to the bare-minimum, last-resort nature of Dibao.

By design, Dibao's implementation is decentralized despite its central regulations. Local governments set and adjust their own Dibao lines that reflect the local minimum living standards and are subject to local fiscal capacity, yielding wide variations in Dibao lines across localities. As shown in Figure 3.3, in December 2014, overall, the Dibao lines of the eastern region were higher than those of the central region, while the western region had the lowest Dibao lines. However, within each region, the Dibao lines varied substantially across provinces and urban–rural areas, with urban lines much higher than rural lines. Further, within the urban areas of each province, the capital cities typically had higher Dibao lines than those in other cities, although selected developed cities other than capital cities set their Dibao lines even higher. Sometimes Dibao

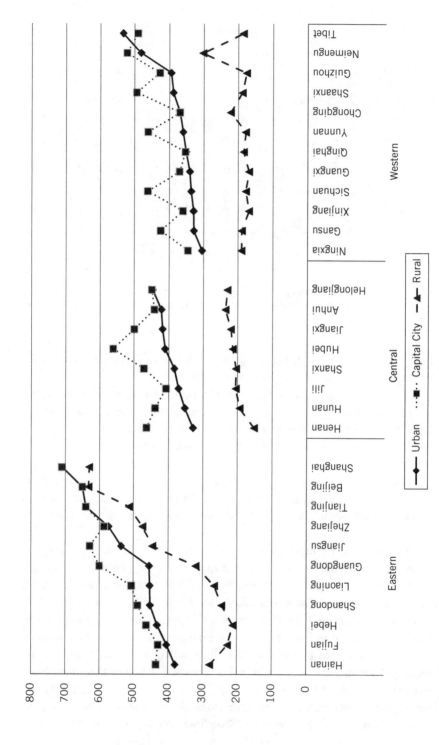

Figure 3.3: Variations in provincial average Dibao lines by region, December 2014 (monthly yuan). Source: Ministry of Civil Affairs (various years).

lines even varied across districts within a given city. For example, Hammond (2011) found substantial variations in Dibao standards across various districts of Dalian.

As pointed out by Umapathi, Wang, and O'Keefe (2013), much of this variation is due to the different approaches adopted to develop and adjust Dibao lines, under the broad national guidelines that permit substantial local discretion. Some localities, such as Beijing, Shanghai, Hebei, and Chongqing, used household surveys to gauge necessary subsistence-level food and non-food expenses and set the Dibao lines accordingly. Other localities, such as Fujian and Hangzhou, rather arbitrarily relied on the local minimum wage to set the local urban Dibao line at 30 to 40% of the minimum wage and then set the rural Dibao line at 60% of the urban line. The majority of localities, such as Anhui, Inner Mongolia, and Shandong, used either the Engel coefficient approach or the proportion of local per capita income or consumption to set Dibao lines. The choice of these different methods, as well as annual adjustments of the Dibao lines, has been driven primarily by local economic conditions and fiscal capacities, with wealthier localities setting Dibao lines at higher levels and adjusting them more substantially than less wealthy ones.

ELIGIBILITY, MEANS TESTING, AND BENEFIT LEVELS

As a strictly means-testing program, Dibao conducts two tests for benefit eligibility (Hong, 2005a). The first is a financial investigation. The value of an eligible family's total financial resources, including income and assets, must be below the local Dibao line for the family to be eligible to receive Dibao benefits. This program adopts a very inclusive income definition to decide each family's eligibility. Household income includes cash income from any source, including earnings, social benefits, private transfers, savings, and stocks. However, due to difficulties of income measurement, some other indicators, such as financial assets, employment, health status, and housing conditions, are also considered (Chen, Ravallion, & Wang, 2006; Du & Park, 2007; Hong, 2005a). Many localities also take into consideration ownership of durable goods, such as a vehicle, motorcycle, or air conditioner.

The second eligibility test concerns household registration status (Hukou) and family formation. Only members who have official local Hukou are eligible. This effectively excludes the millions of rural-to-urban migrants from this program, despite recent initiatives toward balancing the urban–rural benefit levels and removing some of the barriers for migrants to access Dibao and other benefits.

Because the Dibao benefit is meant to bring family income up to the Dibao line level, the actual benefit levels in both urban and rural areas were lower than the Dibao lines, accounting for about 60 to 80% of Dibao lines during the past few years. Figure 3.4 shows the trends in average urban and rural Dibao benefit

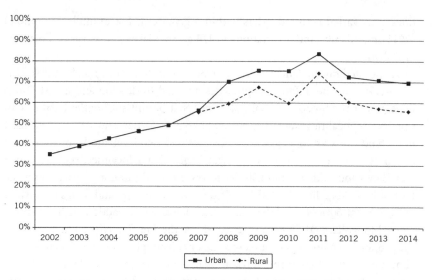

Figure 3.4. Urban and rural average benefit levels as a percentage of Dibao lines (%).
Sources: Average benefit levels from Ministry of Civil Affairs (2002–2014). Their share in Dibao lines was then calculated (Ministry of Civil Affairs, 2002–2014).

levels as a percentage of Dibao lines since their respective national implementations (urban data are available since 2002).

Urban benefit levels as a percentage of Dibao lines increased gradually, from 35% in 2002 to 49% in 2006, and then rose sharply to 70% by 2008. Its growth slowed during the next few years, reaching 75% by 2010. After a surge to 84% in 2011, it dropped again to hover around 71% during 2012–2014. The rural benefit level as a percentage of Dibao lines was 55% in 2007 when it was nationally implemented. It quickly increased to 67% by 2009, dropped to 60% in 2010, and then rose sharply again to 74% in 2011. Since then, it has decreased significantly to hover around 58%, reaching 56% by 2014.

It is hard to explain the exact reasons for changes in these trends, as they are a reflection of several factors, including how far below the Dibao line recipients' incomes were, and how stringent or generous the means-testing process was in each year and across localities. The changes could also reflect macroeconomic development patterns and the determination and willingness of central and local governments to fully finance Dibao.

Strict means testing in Dibao is mandated across localities, but local departments of civil affairs and their officials have ample room for deciding how to carry out the means-testing procedures. While there has been no systematic research on the decentralized means-testing procedures used and how they affect benefit adequacy and service delivery in Dibao, existing qualitative data offer a glimpse into the extent of such variations and how it might be linked to the determination of benefits received by Dibao beneficiaries. Some localities have requirements regarding work ability, asset ownership, and family formation, while others rely more heavily on income information (Solinger, 2010, 2011; Solinger & Hu, 2012). Some routinely use public display of recipient name lists, while others use the lists only sporadically. Even within the same city or district, determination of Dibao eligibility and benefit level can vary to a great extent depending on the procedures used and stringency of local officials administering the procedures (Han, 2012). Solinger (2011) discovered huge gaps in Dibao benefit levels across wealthy and poor districts in Wuhan, even after taking living costs into consideration.

Such variations tend to be more substantial in rural areas than in urban areas, given the greater challenges involved in monitoring the rural Dibao implementation process. Fieldwork done by World Bank research teams revealed that village leaders and representatives often play an important role in identifying and screening potential Dibao beneficiaries. Some villages do not even solicit applications publicly but rather rely on identification and invitation only. This practice is based on the assumption that these village leaders and representatives have sufficient knowledge of the economic conditions and needs of local households and can effectively identify those individuals most in need (Golan, Sicular, & Umapathi, 2014; World Bank, 2011). While this practice also exists in some urban communities, it is much more common in rural than in urban areas. It is, however, deeply flawed and has plenty of room for corruption and inefficiency. Recent efforts to standardize Dibao implementation procedures put forth by the central government were partly aimed to address such variations and inefficiencies.

It is important to understand Dibao's local implementation in the broader context of China's decentralized political system. As pointed out by Wong (2012), with its bottom-heavy administrative structure, China is among the most decentralized countries in the world. Nearly all public services, including basic education, healthcare, social security, and infrastructure, are the responsibilities of local governments at the lower levels. Dibao is one of these most fundamental programs concerning citizen livelihood. This decentralized system leads to much freedom and creativity in local policies and programs, as demonstrated by local Dibao experimentation and initiatives, but it also breeds fragmentation and imbalance, as reflected in the huge variations in Dibao thresholds, eligibility rules, screening procedures, and benefit levels (Boermel, 2011; Cook, 2011; Guan & Xu, 2011).

FINANCING AND EXPENDITURES

The central government requires local governments to commit a budget to the Dibao program, but also provides financial support to localities with financial difficulty (Gustafsson & Gang, 2013; Leung, 2003, 2006; State Council

Information Office, 2004). Since its nationwide implementation in both urban and rural areas, the central government has offered substantial financial subsides to localities to ensure funding for Dibao, especially in less developed regions and provinces that have limited fiscal capacity and greater need for Dibao support. The central government estimates an annual budget for Dibao subsidies on the basis of total revenue and the increases in Dibao thresholds. This budget typically grows every year. It then determines the amount to be transferred to each province based on a formula taking into consideration the number of beneficiaries, management performance, and financial capacity of the provinces.

At the local level, the departments of civil affairs propose an annual budget based on previous and anticipated numbers of beneficiaries and thresholds. This budget is then presented to the departments of finance, statistics, and prices for comments and feedback. The revised budget is submitted to the local people's congress for consideration and approval. In practice, as is the case for most other budget items, typically the local party secretary or head of government makes the final decision. After a budget is approved, the local departments of civil affairs usually stick to it, even if they need to withhold benefits from some eligible families to stay within the budget or provide extra benefits to beneficiaries toward the end of the year in the form of "festival subsidies" to exhaust the budget. They do so for fear that their higher-ups might think that their budget was poorly done and thus give them unfavorable job ratings or distrust their future budget proposals.

Figure 3.5 shows the trends in total government expenditures on urban and rural Dibao since their respective national implementations and the shares of expenditures contributed by central and local governments. The total government expenditures on both urban and rural Dibao programs kept increasing over time, with the rural total expenditure surpassing the urban total expenditure in 2011. In both urban and rural areas, since 2009, central transfers doubled or nearly tripled local funding for Dibao, manifesting the strong financial commitment of the central government to the Dibao program on the one hand and the lack of fiscal capacity in many localities on the other.

Specifically, the total expenditure on urban Dibao increased from a mere 1.4 billion yuan in 1999, when it was nationally implemented, to 10.9 billion yuan in 2002, 22.4 billion yuan in 2006, and 39 billion yuan in 2008. While data on the central–local shares of funding are not available for these earlier years, since 2009, the central government has continuously covered between two thirds and three quarters of the total urban Dibao expenditures, with local governments paying for the remaining portions. In 2014, the total expenditure on urban Dibao was 72 billion yuan, with the central government contributing 52 billion yuan and local governments contributing 20 billion yuan.

The total expenditure on rural Dibao had a much steeper increase curve since its national implementation in 2007, and central government transfers have played an increasingly dominating role since 2009. In 2007, the total expenditure

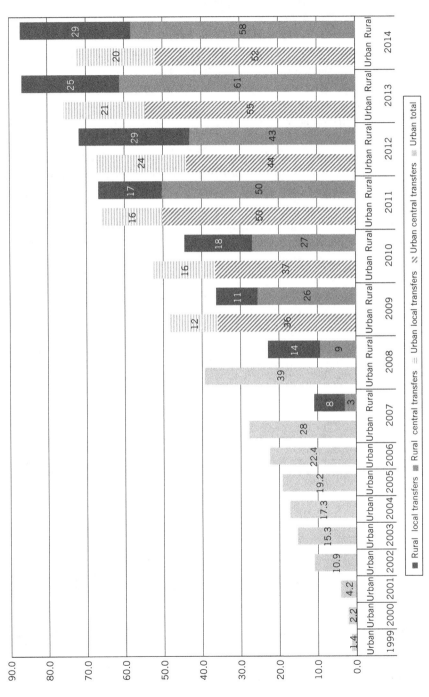

Figure 3-5. Total government expenditures on urban and rural Dibao and central–local transfers (billion yuan). Source: Author's calculations from Ministry of Civil Affairs (1999–2014).

on rural Dibao was 11 billion yuan, with the central government contributing 3 billion yuan and local governments shouldering 8 billion yuan. By 2009, the total rural Dibao expenditure reached 37 billion yuan but the central–local shares shifted, with the central government contributing 26 billion yuan and local governments contributing 11 billion yuan. This pattern largely continued. Since 2011, the total expenditure on rural Dibao has surpassed that on urban Dibao, with the central government covering about two thirds of the total cost. By 2014, the total rural Dibao expenditure reached 87 billion yuan, with the central government contributing 58 billion yuan and local governments contributing 29 billion yuan.

The increasingly substantial proportions of central funding for Dibao reflect how the heavy responsibilities borne by local governments are constrained by their circumscribed expenditure authority and decision making in the Chinese fiscal and administrative structure (Wong, 2012). As discussed in Chapter 2, the central government makes virtually all decisions regarding service provision in basic education, healthcare, and social welfare, with prescribed guidelines for service standards. Meanwhile, taxing is controlled by the central government, while local governments have no power to levy taxes or set tax bases or rates. As a result, many local-government expenditures rely on transfers from the central government, as is the case for Dibao, especially in medium-sized and small cities and inland provinces (Umapathi et al., 2013).

Did the changes in total Dibao expenditures keep pace with the changes in China's gross domestic product (GDP)? Figure 3.6 presents the respective urban

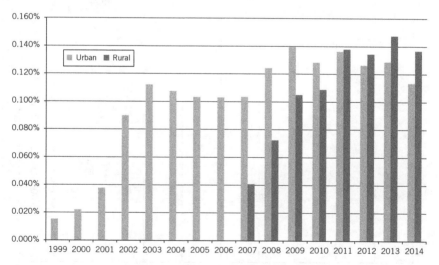

Figure 3.6. Urban and rural Dibao expenditures as a percentage of GDP (%). Sources: Author's calculations from Ministry of Civil Affairs (1999–2014) and National Bureau of Statistics (1999–2014b).

and rural Dibao expenditures as a percentage of GDP since their national implementations. Overall, both urban and rural Dibao expenditures accounted for a very small proportion of GDP, reaching less than 0.15% respectively even at their highest levels. This low proportion manifests the marginal role designated for social assistance in China's economic and social policies. However, Dibao expenditures as a percentage of GDP have increased over time, most notably in rural areas. Indeed, rural Dibao expenditures as a percentage of GDP have surpassed the urban ones during the past few years.

Specifically, total urban Dibao expenditures accounted for only about 0.02% of GDP when it was implemented nationwide in 1999. It then jumped from nearly 0.04% in 2001 to 0.09% in 2002, maintaining an average of about 0.11% during the next 5 years. Since 2008, the total urban Dibao expenditures as a share of GDP hovered around 0.13% but declined to 0.11% by 2014. Total rural Dibao expenditures accounted for 0.04% of GDP when it was implemented nationally in 2007. It then kept rising to 0.14% by 2011 and has since fluctuated somewhat, peaking at 0.15% in 2013 and then dropping back to 0.14% in 2014.

In the international comparative context, China spends relatively less on social safety net programs than many other countries. According to estimates by the Asian Development Bank (ADB) (2009), China spent a total of 0.7% of its GDP on social safety net programs in 2009, among which 0.25% was spent on urban and rural Dibao, according to Figure 3.5. This was substantially lower than the average of 1.6% among developing countries (the median was 1.1%) and the Organisation for Economic Co-operation and Development (OECD) average of 2.9% (country data are from 2010–2014 depending on data availability) (World Bank, 2015).

POPULATION COVERAGE AND BENEFICIARIES

Dibao's population coverage in both urban and rural areas increased rapidly during the early stages but has leveled off in recent years. Figure 3.7 presents the trends in the total numbers of Dibao recipients and as a percentage of the respective urban and rural populations. The number of urban Dibao recipients increased from 0.8 million in 1996 to 2.7 million in 1999 when it was nationally implemented, and then to 20.6 million in 2002. Since then it has fluctuated, peaking at 23.5 million in 2009 but declining to 18.8 million by 2014. Its share in the total urban population rose from 0.2% in 1996 to 0.6% in 1999 and peaked at 4.3% in 2003. Since then, it has been declining gradually and reached 2.5% in 2014.

The number of rural Dibao recipients grew much more rapidly as compared to the urban trend, especially since its national implementation in 2007. It increased from 3.0 million in 2001 to 15.9 million in 2006 and reached 35.7 million in

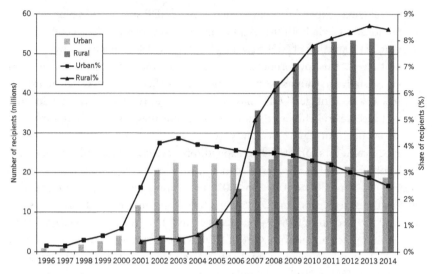

Figure 3.7. Total numbers of Dibao recipients (million persons) and as a percentage of respective urban and rural populations. Sources: Author's calculations from Ministry of Civil Affairs (1996–2014) and National Bureau of Statistics (1996–2014b).

2007. Since then, its growth has continued at a slower pace, peaking at 53.9 million or 8.6% of the rural population in 2013 but falling slightly to 52.1 million or 8.4% of the rural population in 2014.

What are the basic characteristics of the Dibao recipients? As shown in Figure 3.8, in 2014, 63% of all urban Dibao recipients were working-age adults. Among them, only 2% were working full-time or part-time, while 23% held temporary jobs. Most were unemployed and were either not officially registered for their unemployment (21%) or registered unemployed (17%). Among the non-working-age urban Dibao recipients, 21% were children (14% students and 7% non-students) and 17% were older persons. Across the age groups, 8% of urban Dibao recipients were disabled and 42% were women. Among the rural Dibao recipients, 49% were working-age adults, 11% were children, and 40% were older persons. Across the age groups, 9% of rural Dibao recipients were disabled and 35% were women (Ministry of Civil Affairs, 2015a).

Based on more detailed information from the China Household Income Project (CHIP) 2002 and 2007 data, my colleagues and I (Gao, Yang, & Li, 2015) compared the differences in sociodemographic characteristics between families eligible and ineligible for Dibao and between the recipient and non-recipient families within the eligible sample. Overall, we found families ineligible for Dibao to fare much better than the eligible families, and among the eligible sample, the recipient families were somewhat worse off than the non-recipient families. These differences were starker in 2007 than in 2002.

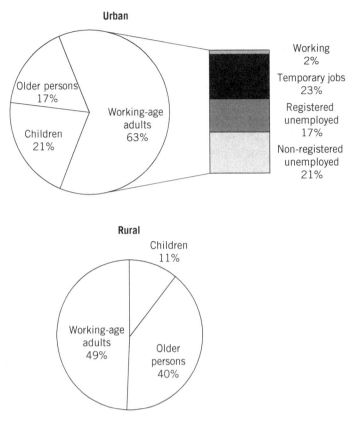

Figure 3.8. Age composition and working status of Dibao recipients, 2014. Source: Ministry of Civil Affairs (2015a).

Specifically, in both 2002 and 2007, heads of households of the ineligible families were better educated, more likely to be employed or retired (as opposed to unemployed) and to have fewer children, and less likely to be from the less developed western region than those of the eligible families. Among the eligible sample, in 2002, recipient families were more likely to be ethnic minority, while in 2007, recipient families were more likely to have a less educated or unemployed head of household and less likely to be from the eastern region than non-recipient families. As expected, in both years, recipient families had significantly lower pre-Dibao household income than their non-recipient peers.

SUMMARY AND IMPLICATIONS

Using administrative data to track Dibao's development over time, this chapter shows that both urban and rural Dibao have undergone significant expansions in their thresholds, benefit levels, expenditures, population coverage, and number of beneficiaries, with the expansions occurring at a faster pace and in more dramatic fashion in rural than in urban areas. However, Dibao lines remain low relative to average consumption levels, manifesting Dibao's fundamental role as a last-resort, bare-minimum safety net program. Dibao's means-testing procedures and benefit levels varied substantially across localities, highlighting both the autonomy enjoyed by local governments in implementing Dibao and the unequal treatment of low-income families in different localities, especially in rural areas where monitoring tends to be more difficult.

Despite the decentralized implementation and requirement for local governments to commit to a budget, Dibao expenditures have been heavily subsidized by the central government. Since 2009, for both urban and rural Dibao, central funding has been double or nearly triple the amount of local funding, demonstrating the strong financial commitment of the central government to the Dibao program on the one hand and the lack of fiscal capacity in many localities on the other. Dibao's population coverage in both urban and rural areas increased rapidly during the early stages of their implementation but has leveled off in recent years. In 2014, Dibao covered 18.8 million urban residents and 52.1 million rural residents, or 2.5% of the urban population and 8.4% of the rural population. Most Dibao recipients are working-age adults, and substantial portions of Dibao recipients are older persons and children.

These trends and patterns reflect broader sociopolitical contexts and have important implications. First and foremost, as was also evident in Chapter 2, the tension and dilemma between central regulation and decentralized implementation are reflected in every aspect of the Dibao program and remain a major challenge as the central government moves toward providing more funding and standardizing Dibao thresholds and procedures. The central government may need to shoulder even greater financial responsibilities if it seeks to diminish and eliminate differences in Dibao lines between urban–rural areas and across localities. Meanwhile, local governments will still be responsible for means testing and determining eligibility and benefit amounts. This dual dynamic could create tension in central control versus local autonomy, which could in turn hinder Dibao's implementation and further expansion.

Second, the faster growth and more significant expansions in rural than in urban Dibao highlight a shift in focus of the Dibao program. As Solinger (2015b) acutely observed, it might be that social unrest among the poor is no longer a major threat to political stability in urban areas, as was the case during the late 1990s and early 2000s, but more of a concern in rural areas. Based on empirical analysis using the China Family Panel Studies (CFPS) 2010 data, my colleague and I (Huang & Gao, 2015) found that receiving Dibao was associated with stronger regime support among rural beneficiaries but not among their urban peers. This trend is likely to continue in the near future as the government works to build and expand a broader rural social benefit system including both social insurance and public assistance. Whether there will be complaints among the urban poor and about the many challenges faced by rural Dibao—such as conducting more accurate means testing and avoiding various forms of mis-targeting—remains to be seen.

4

TARGETING PERFORMANCE

Dibao is a means-tested social assistance program targeting the very poor. Does it reach its intended population? Do the beneficiaries receive the full amounts of entitled benefits? What individual, family, and policy contextual factors are associated with or predictive of Dibao receipt? This chapter evaluates Dibao's targeting performance in two aspects: population targeting and benefit targeting. *Population targeting* captures the proportion of the program's target population who are actual beneficiaries. If a large fraction of program beneficiaries are indeed eligible, the program can be considered to be well population-targeted. *Benefit targeting* refers to the gap between the entitled benefit amount and actual receipt amount, or the benefit gap. A well benefit-targeted program would concentrate total benefits among the target group and deliver the full or majority amounts of entitled benefits to them.

Despite the multiple efforts to enhance means testing and targeting performance of similar cash transfer programs, most poor families around the world still remain outside social assistance programs, especially in lower-income countries. Across low- and lower-middle-income countries, only about one quarter of the poorest quintile is covered by social safety net programs, while that share is higher at 64% among upper-middle-income countries. This under-coverage is especially serious in Sub-Saharan Africa and South Asia, where most of the global poor live, and more challenging among the urban poor than in rural areas of developing countries (World Bank, 2015). Against this broad backdrop, this chapter focuses on Dibao's targeting performance but places it in the international comparative context whenever possible.

TARGETING, MEANS TESTING, AND POVERTY REDUCTION

Before examining the population and benefit targeting performance of Dibao, it is worth discussing the intertwined relations among targeting, means testing, and poverty reduction. Across social assistance programs around the world, targeting is closely related to the rules and procedures adopted by each country and program for means testing. Usually, more stringent means testing leads to better targeting performance, but at higher administrative and social costs. It has higher administrative costs because more personnel and procedures are involved in the means-testing process; it has higher social costs because a stringent process usually involves more disclosure of private information (in terms of both income and assets as well as other family circumstances, such as health condition and family relations), greater peer pressure, and more stigma and shame for the applicants.

Another important cost could be that poverty is actually reduced less due to better targeting and narrower population coverage as a result of more stringent means testing. As Soares, Ribas, and Osório (2010) revealed, cash transfer programs often face a trade-off between better targeting and extending coverage. In contrasting Brazil's Bolsa Família Program with Mexico's Oportunidades Program, both large conditional cash transfer (CCT) programs aiming to support the poor, they found that Oportunidades had better population-targeting performance than Bolsa Família, but at the price of covering fewer households and having a smaller overall anti-poverty impact. Indeed, as Ravallion (2009) pointed out, good targeting coupled with small population coverage often leads to limited poverty reduction, typically the primary goal of such social assistance programs.

Within a given budgetary framework, many countries try to strike a balance between expanding population coverage and providing more adequate transfers to a smaller group of the poor (World Bank, 2015). In reality, it is often a trade-off determined by each country's social value system and political environment (Barrientos, 2013; Umapathi et al., 2013). In the Chinese context, based on simulation analysis using the China Household Income Project (CHIP) 2007–2009 data, Golan, Sicular, and Umapathi (2014) discovered that expanding rural Dibao's population coverage has more potential to reduce poverty than increasing transfer amounts, even after taking into consideration imperfect targeting and local variations in thresholds and transfer amounts.

Across countries, the take-up rate for social assistance is often low compared with that for other types of social benefits. Benefit generosity is also lower in developing than in developed countries, with the median program adding only 10 to 20% to pre-transfer consumption of their beneficiaries in developing countries (Grosh, del Ninno, Tesliuc, & Ouerghi, 2008). Both the low take-up rate and low benefit level have limited the anti-poverty effectiveness of social assistance programs.

POPULATION TARGETING

A detailed and accurate analysis of population coverage and targeting performance of Dibao, as is the case for any other social assistance programs, relies on well-designed, nationally representative, large-scale household survey data that are able to capture the income dynamics and social welfare participation of poor families. In China, a growing number of large-scale household survey data sets in recent years has enabled increasing empirical research to offer insights into the targeting performance of Dibao. However, the differences in the design, sampling, and measures of these data sets also lead to different estimates. In this and the following sections, I present the findings from various studies based on different data sources and summarize the key lessons from these findings.

In the international literature as well as in the literature on Dibao, the most widely used approach to measure population targeting has been to estimate leakage and mis-targeting rates (Cornia & Stewart, 1993), which, respectively, reflect the exclusion and inclusion errors in the population coverage of social assistance programs (see, for example, Du & Park, 2007; Gao, Garfinkel, & Zhai, 2009; Gao, Zhai, Yang, & Li, 2014; Gustafsson & Deng, 2011; Han & Xu, 2013, 2014; Soares et al., 2010). Specifically, the *leakage rate* (i.e., exclusion error rate) refers to the proportion of those who are eligible for benefits but do not receive benefits. The *mis-targeting rate* (i.e., inclusion error rate) measures the share of ineligible recipients in all recipients.

Another approach to measure population targeting, however, is much less used and can add important insights into the targeting performance of social assistance programs. This approach aims to capture the share of cash transfers going to the poorest income groups (usually deciles or quintiles) as well as the concentration index of cash transfers (Coady, Grosh, & Hoddinott, 2004; Ravallion, 2009). If targeting is effective, then the share of cash transfers going to the bottom income groups should be higher than that going to higher income groups, and the concentration index should be more negative, indicating more progressive redistribution of the cash transfers.

Based on both sets of measures, Dibao has notable population-targeting errors and has much room for improvement. However, Chen, Ravallion, and Wang (2006) argued that, despite the existence of these errors, based on international standards, Dibao's population-targeting performance is quite good for a means-tested public assistance program. This highlights the universal challenge faced by social assistance programs to balance targeting and anti-poverty performance.

PARTICIPATION VERSUS ELIGIBILITY RATE

Using large-scale household survey data, a set of studies estimated and con-trasted Dibao's participation and eligibility rates. In survey data, if any member of a household reported receiving any Dibao benefit, the household is considered to be a Dibao participating household. The participation rate is then the propor-tion of Dibao beneficiaries in the sample. Dibao eligibility is estimated on the basis of whether self-reported household income is below the local Dibao line. Any family whose per capita income is below the local Dibao line is considered eligible, and the proportion of eligible families in the sample is the estimated eligibility rate. A gap between the participation and eligibility rates discloses the existence of targeting errors.

It is important to note that estimation of the two rates, especially the eligi-bility rate, depends to a large extent on how Dibao participation and income are measured in the surveys. First, typically surveys use an annual accounting period (e.g., Did any member of your household receive Dibao during the last year? What was your total household income last year?), while in reality Dibao application and eligibility screening is done on a monthly, quarterly, or biannual basis. The discrepancy between the two may not be large but does exist.

Second, and much more complicated, is how income is defined and measured in Dibao's implementation process and across various surveys. In practice, Dibao applicants are expected to report all sources of family income, but there is good reason to suspect that certain income sources, especially the irregular ones such as income from odd jobs and support from family and friends, are concealed. In surveys, income may be asked about in one global question (e.g., What was your total household income last year?) or in great detail, capturing itemized income sources which are then summed to measure total household income. As a general rule, even for the same family, the more exhaustive survey questions are about income, the higher the resulting total household income. Needless to say, the two approaches—and any approach in between—would yield drastically different measurements of income and thus very different estimates of Dibao eligibility.

Meanwhile, it is possible that income reported in surveys is more accurate than that reported by Dibao applicants in reality. After all, surveys usually prom-ise the protection of respondent privacy, and in most cases, survey results do not affect the benefit eligibility or program participation of respondents. In reality, however, it is reasonable to expect that applicants underreport income in order to qualify for Dibao benefits, especially when means testing is not strictly enforced or has loopholes. For example, fieldwork in Dalian revealed deliberate under-reporting of family income by some Dibao applicants in an effort to obtain assis-tance (Yang & Ge, 2002). Such underreporting can backfire and deprive eligible applicants of their entitled benefits if disclosed by peers or uncovered by local authorities. Unfortunately, it is difficult and even impossible to have solid estimates of the extent of income underreporting in the Dibao application process.

For example, Xu (2013) used two income definitions to estimate Dibao eligibility based on a sample of Dibao families from three cities (Baotou, Changsha, and Jinan) in 2012 and generated different results. The first definition used was a comprehensive measure of household income capturing all income sources of a household (referred to as "comprehensive definition"). The second was a definition more realistically used in the Dibao application and screening process (referred to as "administrative definition"), excluding from the first definition income earned by non-Dibao members of the household, income from relatives and friends, and other informal or irregular income. Table 4.1 shows that the Dibao eligibility rate based on the administrative definition was consistently higher than that based on the comprehensive definition, revealing the difference made by income definitions used in estimating the population-targeting performance of such means-tested cash transfer programs.

One intriguing finding in this table is that there seemed to be a correlation between the city Dibao line and the discrepancy between the estimated shares of Dibao-eligible families based on the comprehensive income definition (which assumed full disclosure of family income by Dibao applicants) and administrative income definition (which assumed concealing of certain income sources). The discrepancy appeared to be larger when the city had a low Dibao line, with a difference of 13 percentage points in Changsha, the city with the lowest Dibao line among the three sampled cities, as compared to 8 and 6 percentage points in Jinan and Baotou, respectively, whose Dibao lines were higher. This suggests that Dibao applicants might be more likely to conceal any additional income in order to become eligible for Dibao when the local assistance level is low. It could be that cities with low Dibao lines are of lower economic development levels and have fewer job opportunities, so that poor families are more reliant on Dibao

Table 4.1. Discrepancy in Estimated Dibao Eligibility Rates Based on Different Income Definitions

City	Dibao Line (per capita monthly yuan)	Estimated Dibao Eligibility Rates Based on Two Income Definitions (%)		Discrepancy (b) − (a)
		(a) Comprehensive Definition	(b) Administrative Definition	
Changsha	350	57	70	13
Jinan	450	81	89	8
Baotou	505	90	96	6

Source: Results are from Xu (2013) using survey data collected among 2,810 Dibao families from three cities (Changsha, Jinan, and Baotou) in 2012.

and more motivated to become eligible for it. It could also be that government officials in cities with low Dibao lines are more stringent in determining Dibao eligibility and dispersing Dibao benefits, thus making Dibao benefits more competitive among those who apply for it.

Figure 4.1 presents estimates of urban Dibao participation and eligibility rates based on several large-scale household survey data sets. Across the studies, all estimated a substantially higher participation rate than the eligibility rate, suggesting that urban Dibao had broader population coverage than intended in the study years. However, this may be explained by the discrepancy in income measurements used in surveys and in Dibao's implementation process as discussed earlier and further elaborated later in the chapter.

Specifically, using the CHIP 2002 and 2007 urban surveys, my colleagues and I (Gao, Yang, et al., 2015) found that Dibao's participation rate was 3.7% in 2002 and 4.0% in 2007, both close to the official population coverage rates presented in Chapter 3 (Figure 3.7, 4.1% and 3.8%, respectively). This consistency reinforces the confidence in the quality and national representativeness of the CHIP data. The estimated eligibility rate was 2.3% in 2002 and 1.7% in 2007, much lower than the estimated participation rates, especially in 2007. This is most likely because of the extensive income questions asked in the CHIP survey, which yielded higher income levels than families might actually disclose in the Dibao application process.

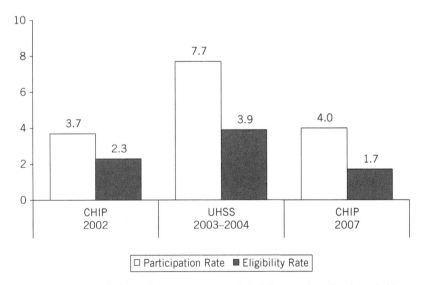

Figure 4.1. Estimates of urban Dibao participation and eligibility rates based on household survey data (%). Sources: Results for 2002 and 2007 are from Gao, Yang, and Li (2015) using the China Household Income Project (CHIP) urban survey data. Results for 2003–2004 are from Chen, Ravallion, and Wang (2006) using the Urban Household Short Survey (UHSS) collected in 35 largest cities.

As a survey that specializes in household income and consumption, CHIP contains particularly rich income information as compared to other household surveys in China. In this study, my colleagues and I calculated total household disposable income from the sum of wages, business income, property income, and pre-Dibao transfer income from all family members. If a household's per capita disposable income was lower than the local Dibao line, then the household was considered eligible for Dibao. However, many other surveys do not itemize these income components, leading the respondents to report only the most apparent and regular income sources. In reality, it is also possible that Dibao applicants underreport or conceal income from business, property, transfers, and even wages from underground or irregular jobs. This may help partly explain the lower estimated eligibility rate than the participation rate.

Using a different data source, Chen et al. (2006) estimated a similar gap between the participation and eligibility rates in urban Dibao. The data set they used was the Urban Household Short Survey (UHSS) for 2003–2004, which is a subset of the National Bureau of Statistics's regular Urban Household Survey (UHS). The UHSS contained data collected among 76,000 households in China's 35 largest cities. It is important to note that these large cities tend to have higher Dibao assistance lines and broader population coverage than smaller cities. The authors found the participation rate in this sample to be 7.7%, nearly doubling the estimated eligibility rate of 3.9%. In this study, income was measured on the basis of a global question, "What was your total household income last year?" which yielded a much higher eligibility rate than that based on the CHIP data. However, this might be partly due to the fact that the sample in this study was from the large cities that offered more generous Dibao benefits than the smaller cities in the CHIP survey. Indeed, using the same data source, Wang (2006) found that a 15% increase in city Dibao line would result in a 35% increase in the eligible rate, while a 15% decrease in city Dibao line would lead to a 22% decline in the eligible rate.

The estimated gap between participation and eligibility rates for rural Dibao is reversed from the urban pattern. Only one existing study provided empirical evidence on this topic for rural Dibao. As shown in Figure 4.2, using CHIP 2007–2009 rural data, Golan et al. (2014) estimated the Dibao participation rate to increase from 1.9% in 2007 to 2.0% in 2008 and 3.0% in 2009. These rates, however, were substantially lower than those based on official data for the same provinces in the CHIP sample. The official data showed a rural Dibao participation rate of 4.6% in 2008 and 5.6% in 2009 (the data for 2007 were unavailable), both more than doubling the estimated participation rates based on CHIP data. This is possibly because the rural households in the CHIP sample were better off than the national average. It could be particularly difficult to capture the extremely poor in the rural population in surveys, given their meager living conditions and reservation about participating in such projects. Typically, rural surveys rely more on the assistance of local officials and community leaders than urban ones do, and it is reasonable to expect that these local officials and leaders try to avoid extremely poor households as survey targets to "save face" for the locality.

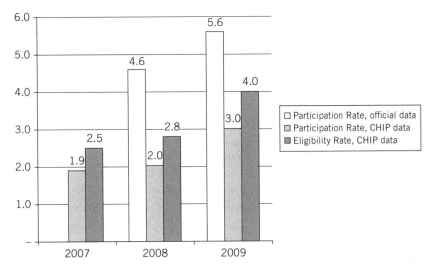

Figure 4.2. Estimates of rural Dibao participation and eligibility rates based on official and household survey data (%). Source: Golan, Sicular, and Umapathi (2014). Official data are from the Ministry of Civil Affairs and National Bureau of Statistics (NBS) and household data are from the China Household Income Project (CHIP) 2007–2009 rural surveys. Participation rate based on official data was unavailable in 2007.

In contrast to the urban patterns revealed in empirical research, Golan et al. (2014) showed that the estimated eligibility rate was consistently higher than the participation rate in rural China. In 2007, the estimated eligibility rate was 2.5%, as compared to the participation rate of 1.9%. By 2009, the gap between the two further increased to 4.0% versus 3.0%. This discrepancy may be partly due to the unique challenges in measuring income in rural China—both in surveys and by local Dibao officials—and partly due to the various types of targeting errors discovered by fieldwork in rural Dibao.

On the one hand, rural income has always been harder to capture than urban income because of the irregular nature of rural income. The bulk of income for most rural households is from agricultural income and nonagricultural self-employment, both in cash and in kind. In the CHIP survey, rural household income data were collected using a diary method. The benefit of the diary method is that it reduces recall error. However, it might be difficult for rural residents to keep track of their complex and diverse income sources. Some may even lack the ability or willingness to record such detailed income data. These challenges could be especially prominent for poor and vulnerable families, who tend to have lower incomes as well as lower capacity for recording the information accurately. As a result, more rural families may report income levels below the local Dibao lines, which would make them eligible for Dibao benefits.

On the other hand, as discussed in Chapter 2 and noted by Golan and colleagues (2014), the decentralized implementation of Dibao allows rural officials at the county, township, and village levels considerable discretionary power, leading to several types of targeting errors such as allocating Dibao on the basis of personal connections or relationships (*guanxi bao* or *renqing bao*), cheating (*pian bao*), and mistakes (*cuo bao*). These errors also exist in urban China, but they are more widespread in rural areas given the greater challenges in checks and balances in the rural setting and more discretionary power bestowed to rural Dibao officials than to their urban peers. Rural Dibao applicants tend to be less well-informed about Dibao policies, procedures, and standards than their urban peers. They may also be less willing to complain and have fewer channels for filing grievances about injustice in Dibao implementation.

One other factor that may have contributed to this finding is a data limitation in the income measurement used in this study. The CHIP 2007–2009 rural survey does not contain household-level information on the amount of Dibao transfers, thus limiting the researchers' ability to precisely measure pre-Dibao income and estimate family eligibility for Dibao benefits. The authors used village- and county-level average Dibao transfers to approximate household-level transfers, and the two approaches yielded similar estimates. However, it is important to note the variation in inter-household Dibao transfer amounts, which would lead to somewhat—though not drastically—different eligibility rates at the aggregate level.

LEAKAGE AND MIS-TARGETING RATES

To help better understand Dibao's population-targeting performance, a set of studies used large-scale household survey data sets to estimate Dibao's leakage and mis-targeting rates. As shown in Figure 4.3, across studies and over time, urban Dibao had substantial leakage and mis-targeting rates, suggesting serious challenges in its population-targeting performance. However, such targeting errors are inevitable in unconditional cash transfer (UCT) programs around the world and have been well documented in the international comparative literature (Barrientos, 2013; Coady et al., 2004). Indeed, Dibao's population-targeting performance is deemed better than most other UCT programs around the world, especially in low- and middle-income countries (Chen et al., 2006).

Specifically, using the CHIP 2002 and 2007 urban survey data, my colleagues and I (Gao, Yang, et al., 2015) estimated that 54% of eligible families were not covered by Dibao in 2002. This leakage rate declined but remained substantial at 42% in 2007. The estimated mis-targeting rate was much higher than the leakage rate in both years, reaching 74% in 2002 and 76% in 2007, indicating that around three quarters of urban Dibao recipients in the CHIP sample were actually ineligible. These mis-targeting rates were much higher than those found in other studies, probably because of the much more comprehensive income measure available in the CHIP data, which in turn led to a possible overestimate of the mis-targeting rate.

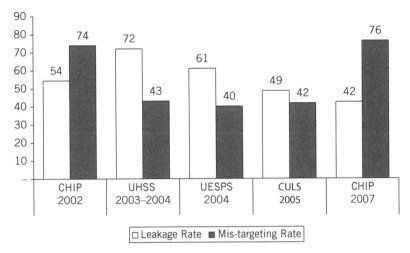

Figure 4.3. Estimates of urban Dibao leakage and mis-targeting rates based on household survey data (%). Sources: Results for 2002 and 2007 are from Gao, Yang, and Li (2015) using the China Household Income Project (CHIP) urban survey data. Results for 2003–2004 are from Chen, Ravallion, and Wang (2006) using the Urban Household Short Survey (UHSS) data collected in 35 largest cities. Results for 2004 are from Wang (2007) using the Urban Employment and Social Protection Survey (UESPS) data collected in 14 cities of various sizes. Results for 2005 are from Du and Park (2007) using the China Urban Labor Survey (CULS) data collected in five big cities (Shanghai, Wuhan, Shenyang, Fuzhou, and Xi'an).

The other three studies reported in Figure 4.3 also showed significant leakage and mis-targeting rates, but with the estimated mis-targeting rate lower than the leakage rate. Using the UHSS data collected from 35 largest cities in 2003–2004, Chen et al. (2006) found that 82% of eligible families were excluded, while 43% of the households who received Dibao were actually ineligible. Using the Urban Employment and Social Protection Survey (UESPS) data collected in 14 cities of various sizes, Wang (2007) found the leakage rate to be 61% and the mis-targeting rate to be 40%. Using the China Urban Labor Survey (CULS) data collected in five big cities (Shanghai, Wuhan, Shenyang, Fuzhou, and Xi'an) in 2005, Du and Park (2007) found that 49% of eligible families were excluded from Dibao while 42% of the actual beneficiaries were not qualified.

The estimated leakage and mis-targeting rates in rural Dibao are mostly higher than those in urban Dibao, highlighting the additional challenges in population targeting in the rural context. Figure 4.4 presents these estimates from two empirical studies. Using the CHIP 2007–2009 rural survey data, Golan et al. (2014) estimated very high leakage and mis-targeting rates in rural Dibao for all 3 years. Specifically, the leakage rate was 94% in 2007, which dropped slightly to 93% in 2008 and then to 89% in 2009, suggesting that the overwhelming majority of eligible households did not receive Dibao benefits. The estimated mis-targeting rate was equally alarming; it was 94% in 2007 and decreased slightly to

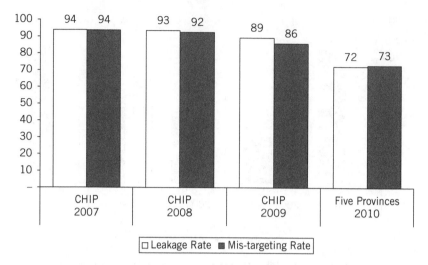

Figure 4.4. Estimates of rural Dibao leakage and mis-targeting rates based on household survey data (%). Sources: Results for 2007–2009 are from Golan, Sicular, and Umapathi (2014) using the China Household Income Project (CHIP) rural survey data. Dibao eligibility was estimated on the basis of household income net of county average Dibao transfer amount. Results for 2010 are from Han and Xu (2014) using data collected among 9,107 rural households in five provinces (Jiangxi, Anhui, Henan, Shaanxi, and Gansu) in central and western China.

92% in 2008 and 86% in 2009, revealing that most rural Dibao beneficiaries were actually ineligible for the benefits.

As noted earlier, these high estimates could be partly due to the unique challenges in collecting rural household income data and partly due to inefficiencies in rural Dibao implementation. As the CHIP rural survey did not ask about the exact Dibao transfer amounts received by the households, the authors used village or county average transfer amounts to impute household-level transfer amounts in order to estimate eligibility. The results using the county average transfer amounts are shown in Figure 4.4; the results using village average transfer amounts are not shown in the figure but are very similar.

In another study, Han and Xu (2014) used data collected among 9,107 rural households in five provinces (Jiangxi, Anhui, Henan, Shaanxi, and Gansu) in central and western China in 2010 and estimated somewhat lower but still substantial leakage and mis-targeting rates. As shown in Figure 4.4, the estimated leakage rate was 72% while the mis-targeting rate was 73%, both revealing significant targeting errors.

Through fieldwork and qualitative interviews with low-income families as well as Dibao officials, researchers have identified several leading factors contributing to the leakage and mis-targeting of Dibao. The most notable factors include inefficient program administration, corruption among local Dibao officials, and stigma associated with receiving the benefits (Golan et al., 2014; Leung, 2006;

Solinger, 2011). Using CULS data and multinomial logit regression models, Du and Park (2007) discovered that, among the extremely poor, income could be used as an effective tool for identifying eligible families and avoiding leakage errors. However, as income increases to higher levels, it becomes much harder to use income as the sole means-testing tool. Other factors, such as employment status and capability as well as health status, can help supplement income information and improve Dibao's targeting performance.

DO DIBAO BENEFITS CONCENTRATE ON THE POOR?

Another set of population-targeting measures focuses on the share of cash transfers going to the poor and the concentration ratio of these cash transfers, which complements the measurements based on leakage and mis-targeting rates and helps offer a more nuanced analysis of population-targeting performance. Empirical evidence shows that, in both urban and rural China, Dibao benefits concentrate among the bottom-income groups, while higher-income groups also benefit from Dibao due to the existence of targeting errors.

In the case of urban Dibao, using the CULS data collected in five big cities, Du and Park (2007) found that Dibao had become the dominant social assistance program in urban China, with the poorest 20% of the population receiving 55% of its transfers in 2001 and more than 80% of Dibao benefits in 2005. Using the UHSS data collected in China's 35 largest cities in 2003–2004, Chen et al. (2006) estimated that 64% of all benefits went to Dibao-eligible families, despite the notable leakage and mis-targeting errors.

In the case of rural Dibao, based on survey data collected among 9,107 rural households in five central and western provinces in 2010, Han and Xu (2014) found that, among the total Dibao benefits delivered to recipient families, only 28% went to those whose family income was below the local Dibao line. The percentage increased to 57% if the national rural poverty line of 2,300 yuan per capita per year was used. In total, the poorest 20% of the sample received 52% of all Dibao benefits, while the richest 20% received less than 2% of all Dibao benefits. The remaining 46% Dibao benefits went to the middle 60% of the income distribution.

My colleague and I (Gao & Riskin, 2009) used CHIP 2002 data to analyze the inequality of distribution of each income source through estimating the concentration index. The concentration index, or concentration ratio, is measured analogously to the Gini coefficient, except that it measures the distribution of an income source over all income recipients rather than only over recipients of that source (which would be a true Gini coefficient). We found that, in urban China, Dibao was the only income source with a negative concentration ratio, suggesting that most of it went to poor households and it was progressively distributed. In rural China, however, Dibao income still had a positive concentration ratio, echoing earlier discussions that the population-targeting performance of rural Dibao was much worse than that of urban Dibao.

BENEFIT TARGETING

Another important aspect of Dibao's targeting performance is benefit target-ing, which refers to whether there is a gap between the entitled benefit amount and actual receipt amount among beneficiaries. The entitled benefit amount is the amount of money that would bring a family's post-transfer income up to the Dibao line level. A narrower benefit gap indicates better benefit-targeting performance, suggesting beneficiaries are receiving most of the benefits they are entitled to. A wider benefit gap, on the other hand, suggests that only a lim-ited amount of benefits are delivered and there are significant benefit-targeting errors.

Existing studies have revealed notable benefit delivery gaps in both urban and rural Dibao. Figure 4.5 presents the received amounts of Dibao benefits and the remaining benefit gaps among eligible families estimated in four empirical studies. The full length of each bar (with the benefit gap stacked on top of the received amount) captures the entitled benefit amount. This figure shows that the entitled urban Dibao benefit amount kept increasing from 2002 to 2007, thanks to the increases in urban Dibao lines, as shown by Figure 3.1 in Chapter 3. The urban benefit amount received by eligible families increased over time, but the remaining benefit gap also kept increasing, although to a lesser extent. The rural benefit gap was narrower than the urban benefit gap, mainly because of the much lower Dibao lines and entitled benefit amounts in rural than in urban areas.

Specifically, in the case of urban Dibao, using NHSS data from 35 largest cit-ies collected in 2003–2004, Wang (2006) found that the average annual Dibao benefits received by eligible families was only 273 yuan, with a wide benefit gap of 620 yuan to bring the annual income of these families to their entitled benefit level of 893 yuan. Using CHIP 2002 and 2007 data, my colleagues and I (Gao, Garfinkel, et al., 2009; Gao, Yang, et al., 2015) found that the average Dibao ben-efit received by eligible families increased from 169 yuan in 2002 to 844 yuan in 2007, a significant increase over the 5-year period. However, the benefit gap also increased during this time, from 510 yuan in 2002 to 628 yuan in 2007, indi-cating somewhat bigger benefit targeting errors over time. Overall, the entitled amount of benefits (as captured by the full length of the bars) kept increasing in urban China from 2002 to 2007, suggesting that more generous Dibao ben-efits brought more transfers to eligible families but also offered more room for benefit-targeting error.

With regard to rural Dibao, based on survey data collected among 9,107 households in five provinces in 2010, Han and Xu (2014) found that the average

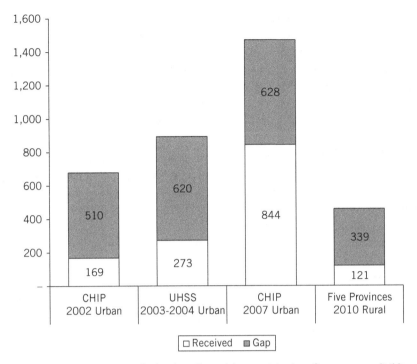

Figure 4.5. Received amounts of Dibao benefits and the remaining benefit gap among eligible families (annual yuan in current year value). Sources: Results for 2002 and 2007 are from Gao, Garfinkel, and Zhai (2009) and Gao, Yang, and Li (2015) using the China Household Income Project (CHIP) urban survey data. Results for 2003–2004 are from Wang (2006) using the Urban Household Short Survey (UHSS) data collected in 35 largest cities. Results for 2010 are from Han and Xu (2014) using data collected among 9,107 rural households in five provinces (Jiangxi, Anhui, Henan, Shaanxi, and Gansu) in central and western China.

Dibao benefit received by eligible families was only 121 annual yuan, while the remaining benefit gap was 339 yuan, 2.8 times that of the actual amount received. The full amount of entitled benefits was 460 yuan, much lower than the entitled amounts in urban areas. Consequently, the rural benefit gap—though substantial, especially relative to the actual amounts received by rural beneficiaries—was still much narrower than the urban benefit gap.

FACTORS PREDICTIVE OF DIBAO RECEIPT AND BENEFIT AMOUNT

Given the significant population- and benefit-targeting errors in both urban and rural Dibao, what factors help decide who do and who do not receive Dibao, and for beneficiaries, how much benefit they receive? Some of these factors, such as personal connections, corruption, and inefficiencies in administration, are intangible and hard to measure through empirical research. Some others, however, can be empirically examined and tested. A growing body of literature has identified some individual, family, and policy contextual factors that are significantly associated with Dibao receipt and the amount of benefits received by beneficiaries (Chen et al., 2006; Du & Park, 2007; Gao, Garfinkel, et al., 2009; Gao, Yang, et al., 2015; Golan et al., 2014; Gustafsson & Deng, 2011; Han & Xu, 2013; Leung, 2006).

Among individual-level factors, for urban Dibao, unemployment, low wages, inadequate pensions, low education, poor health, disability, and old age were identified as the leading factors associated with Dibao receipt as well as the amount of benefit received by beneficiaries. Given the low rates of formal employment and pensions in rural areas, low education, poor health, disability, and old age played more dominating predictive roles in rural than in urban Dibao.

Among family-level factors, across both urban and rural areas, low financial wealth, having a female head of household, large household size, the presence of more members aged 60 or above, and the presence of disabled or chronically ill members were all associated with a higher probability of receiving Dibao and greater amounts of benefit received. For rural Dibao, several additional factors were predictive of Dibao receipt. These included having a household member with a migrant job, having had a death in the family during the past year, and living in a community with more roads covered by asphalt or cement. Having more cultivated land and having a flush toilet, on the other hand, were associated with a lower probability of Dibao receipt (Golan et al., 2014).

Several policy contextual factors have been identified as predictive of both Dibao receipt and the amount of benefits received by families. Most importantly, a more generous Dibao policy, as measured by the local Dibao line, helped increase both the likelihood of Dibao receipt and the amount of benefits received. Among eligible families, those who had higher amounts of entitled benefits usually also received more benefits. Living in a provincial capital city or one with a higher unemployment rate was also associated with a higher probability of Dibao receipt as well as the amount of benefit received by families (Gao, Garfinkel, et al., 2009; Gao, Yang, et al., 2015; Gustafson & Deng, 2011).

SUMMARY AND IMPLICATIONS

This chapter examines the population- and benefit-targeting performance of Dibao as a means-testing social assistance program. Existing evidence indicates that there are substantial targeting errors in both urban and rural Dibao. Estimates based on large-scale household survey data show discrepancies between the Dibao participation rate and eligibility rate. The urban participation rate was estimated to be higher than the eligibility rate, while this pattern was reversed for rural Dibao. These discrepancies may be partly explained by the different income measures used in various surveys as well as in Dibao's actual implementation process, and partly explained by the unique challenges in measuring household income in respective urban and rural settings. Such challenges may be especially prominent in rural areas where incomes are more reliant on agricultural production and more likely to be from irregular sources.

Empirical analyses using various measures of population targeting further revealed substantial leakage and mis-targeting errors in Dibao. Across urban and rural areas, significant portions of eligible families were mistakenly excluded from the Dibao benefit, while some others were mis-targeted or included erroneously in Dibao coverage. The exact extents of these errors vary across estimates based on different data sources and income definitions, but in general, rural Dibao had more severe leakage and mis-targeting errors than urban Dibao, highlighting the greater challenges in checks and balances and the more complex administrative processes in the rural setting. Urban Dibao benefits were also better concentrated among the poor than were rural benefits.

Dibao's benefit-targeting performance also has serious deficits. The urban benefit gap—the difference between the entitled amount and the actual amount received by families—kept increasing, although to a lesser extent over time, especially when compared to the pace of increase in the receipt amount. The rural benefit gap was narrower than the urban one because of the much lower Dibao lines and lower entitled benefit amounts in rural than in urban areas, rather than better benefit-targeting performance per se.

These findings highlight the common challenge of targeting faced by similar means-tested cash transfer programs around the world. Indeed, although Dibao has significant targeting errors, its performance is deemed good or even better than most in the international comparative context (Chen et al., 2006; Coady et al., 2004). It is also important to bear in mind the inevitable trade-off between better targeting and broader coverage. Usually, broader coverage leads to better poverty reduction outcomes, while better targeting does not necessarily lead to the same outcome. Targeting has significant financial and social costs involved, all of which need to be considered in designing more effective strategies for improved targeting performance.

Existing research also revealed a series of individual, family, and policy contextual factors that were associated with Dibao receipt and higher amounts of benefit received. While certain groups are more vulnerable and arguably more deserving than others to receive Dibao support, it is also important to pay attention to those who do not belong to these groups but still have incomes below the local Dibao line. It is possible that these other families have needs or hardships that are difficult to capture through survey data, or are more private and less visible to others. It is also possible that the inefficiencies in Dibao implementation and corruption of local officials shield other risk factors for leakage and mis-targeting. Future research needs to adopt better designs and methodologies to investigate these hidden factors, and future policy changes need to take these additional risk factors into consideration.

Throughout the analysis and discussion, this chapter has also highlighted the challenges in measuring household income accurately through survey data as well as matching the survey data with Dibao's actual implementation process. Moving forward, more in-depth interviews and fieldwork can help provide important insights into the reasons behind the targeting errors and risk factors identified in this chapter, especially in rural areas where existing evidence on Dibao is limited. Meanwhile, it would be enormously helpful to develop well-designed, large-scale longitudinal data collection efforts to enable more nuanced analysis of entry into and exit from Dibao and their associated factors.

5

ANTI-POVERTY EFFECTIVENESS

Dibao's primary goal is to serve as a last resort to poor families through providing monthly cash transfers. How effective has Dibao been in lifting the incomes of recipient families and helping them escape poverty? Does Dibao help narrow the income distribution gap and reduce overall income inequality? Building on the evidence on means testing and targeting performance discussed in Chapter 4, this chapter presents the evidence on Dibao's anti-poverty effectiveness and discusses implications for achieving Dibao's poverty reduction goals.

Internationally, a growing body of experimental and observational studies has shown that cash transfers remain one of the most effective anti-poverty tools, with supportive evidence from around the world and across developing and developed countries. Many of these studies are based on randomized controlled trials (RCTs) and are able to measure the causal and long-term effects of welfare participation (Barrientos, 2013; Grosh et al., 2008; Moffitt, 2003b, 2015; Rawlings & Rubio, 2005; Ziliak, 2009, 2016).

As discussed in this chapter, existing evidence shows that Dibao has helped alleviate poverty among its target population, with a particularly significant effect on reductions in poverty gap and severity. However, Dibao's effectiveness in reducing poverty is limited by its partial coverage and delivery, thus its full potential in combating poverty has not been achieved. I first present descriptive results regarding the income and wealth profiles of Dibao families. I then introduce the poverty measures used in the literature and focus on a thorough investigation of Dibao's anti-poverty effectiveness. I also examine the factors that undermine or contribute to Dibao's anti-poverty effectiveness and discuss policy implications of these findings.

INCOME AND WEALTH PROFILES OF DIBAO FAMILIES

What financial resources do Dibao families have available and how much do they amount to? Before delving into Dibao's effectiveness in reducing poverty, I first present the income and wealth profiles of Dibao families that are documented in existing studies. This set of literature shows that Dibao is the main source of income for most recipient families. While these families have other income sources, they are often of smaller amounts and tend to be irregular. Dibao families also have substantially less wealth than their non-recipient peers.

Based on survey data collected among 2,810 Dibao recipient families in three cities (Jinan, Changsha, and Baotou) in 2012, Xu (2013) reported that Dibao was the primary income source for these families, making up 40% of their total household income. The next largest source of income was wages, presumably earned by non-Dibao-eligible members, which accounted for 33% of family income. Informal support from friends and relatives contributed another 10% of Dibao recipients' family income. Pensions accounted for 8% of total household income, followed by income from private businesses (4%). The remaining 5% of family income was from other sources, such as unemployment benefits and subsidies for disability or veterans. There were some variations in the detailed composition of family income across the three cities in this study, but Dibao remained the primary source of income for these families, and the composition of family income was mostly consistent across cities.

In rural areas, Han and Xu (2014) used data collected among 9,107 rural households in five provinces in central and western China in 2010 and found that Dibao families had substantially lower per capita household disposable income, smaller dwellings, and fewer assets than their non-Dibao recipient peers. Specifically, as shown in Table 5.1, the average annual per capita household disposable income among Dibao families was 2,296 yuan, which was below the 2011 national rural poverty line of 2,300 yuan and accounted for only 42% of average income among non-Dibao families. Dibao families also had somewhat smaller dwellings, averaging 29 square meters as compared to 33 square meters among their non-Dibao peers. Dibao families also had fewer assets or valuable goods, including color TVs, computers, cars, motorcycles, landline or mobile phones, tractors, pedicabs, and harvesting equipment.

These quantitative findings are echoed by evidence from fieldwork and qualitative interview data. For example, Solinger depicted vividly the material hardships experienced by some Dibao recipients across several cities. She described the dwellings in which Dibao recipients resided to be "generally old and dilapidated, tiny and without any decoration, unless a poster or photo on a wall" (Solinger, 2012, p. 1020).

To what extent are Dibao transfers helpful in lifting income levels of recipient families? According to Dibao families themselves, the assistance remains

Table 5.1. Income and Asset Profiles of Rural Dibao and Non-Dibao Families, 2010

	Dibao Families (n = 868)		Non-Dibao Families (n = 8,239)	
	Mean	SD	Mean	SD
Income and Housing				
Per capita disposable income (annual yuan)	2296.23	(1849.87)	5463.90	(5061.97)
Per capita living space (square meters)	22.35	(25.48)	33.16	(25.37)
Asset Ownership				
Color TV	0.68	(0.47)	0.89	(0.31)
Computer	0.02	(0.12)	0.09	(0.28)
Car	0.01	(0.10)	0.05	(0.21)
Motorcycle	0.17	(0.37)	0.40	(0.49)
Landline phone	0.25	(0.43)	0.48	(0.50)
Mobile phone	0.52	(0.50)	0.80	(0.40)
Large tractor	0.01	(0.12)	0.03	(0.16)
Small tractor	0.14	(0.35)	0.29	(0.46)
Pedicab	0.10	(0.30)	0.13	(0.34)
Harvesting equipment	0.00	(0.07)	0.01	(0.11)

Source: Table 1 in Han and Xu (2014), using data collected among 9,107 rural households in five provinces (Jiangxi, Anhui, Henan, Shaanxi, and Gansu) in central and western China in 2010.

limited. In a survey conducted among 1,209 Dibao recipients in six cities in 2007 by researchers from Renmin University of China and commissioned by the Department of Social Assistance of the Ministry of Civil Affairs, when asked whether Dibao benefits were sufficient to cover their basic living expenses, only 3.7% of the respondents said yes. About half (47.9%) considered Dibao benefits barely sufficient, another one third (32.5%) said Dibao benefits were insufficient, and about one sixth (15.4%) considered Dibao benefits far from helping them meeting their basic needs (Han & Guo, 2012).

POVERTY MEASURES AND THRESHOLDS

Most existing studies that have examined Dibao's anti-poverty effectiveness have used a set of the most widely used poverty outcomes, referred to as the Foster–Greer–Thorbecke (FGT) index, which includes the poverty rate, depth, and severity (Foster, Greer, & Thorbecke, 1984). The *poverty rate* is defined as the poverty headcount ratio and is calculated as the share of the population whose income falls below the poverty threshold. The *poverty depth* is measured as the poverty gap ratio, or the income shortfall as a percentage of the poverty line. The *poverty severity* is measured by the squared poverty gap ratio, so more weight is given to the extreme poor among the poor population. These studies compared the pre- and post-Dibao poverty rates, depth, and severity in order to assess the impact of Dibao on poverty reduction.

It is important to note two methodological issues that are central to the estimation of Dibao's anti-poverty effects. First, consistent with the majority of literature on cash transfer programs around the world, especially in developing countries, family income, rather than consumption, has been the basis for estimating poverty outcomes in the Dibao literature. In most data sets concerning China, income data have been much more systematically collected and available than consumption data, making income the most often used definition for measuring poverty in existing studies. This is especially true in the Dibao literature, as Dibao eligibility is determined mainly on the basis of household income level as compared to the local Dibao line.

Second, as in any research on poverty, the estimated poverty outcomes of Dibao depend to a great extent on the poverty threshold adopted. In the Dibao literature, four sets of poverty thresholds have been used. The first set is the World Bank poverty lines of $1, $1.25, or $2 per person per day, based on purchasing power parity (PPP). This set of poverty lines has the advantage of being widely accepted and used in the international comparative literature. Its downside, however, is that such poverty lines are arbitrarily set based on an international standard and do not reflect the huge variations in economic development and living standards in urban and rural China and across its regions and provinces. The $1 and $1.25 per person per day poverty lines also tend to be too low to meet the average living standard in current Chinese society, especially in urban areas.

The second set of poverty thresholds used in the Dibao literature is a national poverty line, either estimated by researchers or set by the government. Specifically, a poverty line developed by Khan (2004) according to the minimum food intake required to sustain energy (i.e., 2,100 kilocalories per person per day) in the Chinese context has been used in several Dibao studies (e.g., Gao, Garfinkel, et al., 2009; Gustafsson & Deng, 2011). In addition, the Chinese government has set a national poverty line for rural areas, which was 1,196 yuan per person per year before 2011 but has been increased to 2,300 yuan per person per year since 2011.

The third set of poverty thresholds is the Dibao line. Set by local governments to determine Dibao eligibility and benefits, the Dibao line reflects the basic livelihood level according to local standards as well as financial capacities of the localities. They vary across regions and provinces, and across cities and counties within provinces. As a result, the Dibao line is a much more localized poverty threshold than the two sets presented earlier. It also serves as a benchmark to judge Dibao's performance. If targeting and benefit delivery were perfect, then Dibao would eliminate poverty completely based on this poverty line. However, this is not the case, as discussed in Chapter 4. Results based on this poverty line thus help reveal the extent to which Dibao reaches its intended policy goal of reducing poverty among its target population. Given the existence of varied local Dibao lines at the city and county level, many researchers often use a simplified Dibao line—calculated as the provincial average Dibao line—to estimate poverty outcomes (Deng & Li, 2010; Li & Yang, 2009).

The last set of poverty thresholds is the relative poverty lines set at certain points (usually 50% or 60% of median income) in the overall societal income distribution. This type of poverty line is much more widely used in developed countries than in developing countries (e.g., Garfinkel, Rainwater, & Smeeding, 2010). However, a few recent studies on Dibao have adopted relative poverty lines to assess Dibao's anti-poverty effectiveness, taking into consideration the overall income distribution of society (Gao, 2013; Gao, Garfinkel, et al., 2009; Golan et al., 2014).

Each of the these poverty thresholds has its own pros and cons. In the next section, I present the existing evidence on Dibao's anti-poverty effectiveness using these different poverty thresholds. The findings, taken together, show that the results largely converge but also reveal some different patterns that reflect the strengths and limitations of the various poverty thresholds.

ANTI-POVERTY EFFECTIVENESS

Dibao's effectiveness in combatting poverty has been extensively examined in the literature, especially in the urban setting. Most existing studies on this topic use large-scale household survey data to gauge family income and poverty status and examine the extent to which Dibao helps alleviate poverty. Both urban and rural Dibao have been found to have a modest impact on reducing poverty, with effects being greater in reducing the poverty gap and severity than the poverty rate. Dibao's anti-poverty effectiveness is more substantial when a lower poverty threshold is used and is most limited when relative poverty lines are adopted, as they are set relative to median income and tend to be much higher than any of the absolute poverty lines.

The first set of studies used the World Bank PPP poverty lines to examine Dibao's anti-poverty effectiveness among eligible families and the general population. This body of research found that Dibao had limited effect on reducing poverty among the general population, but its anti-poverty effectiveness was much more substantial among Dibao's target population, especially in reducing the poverty gap and severity as opposed to the poverty rate.

Using the China Urban Labor Survey (CULS) data collected in five big cities in 2001 and 2005, Du and Park (2007) estimated that Dibao had very limited effects in lowering the poverty rate among the general population. As shown in Figure 5.1, based on the World Bank poverty lines of $1 and $2 per person per

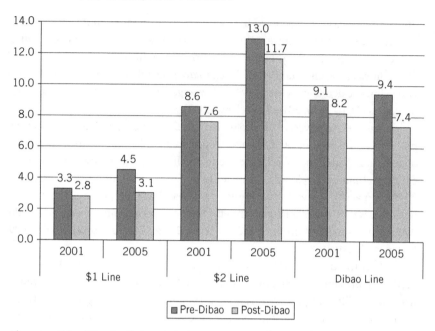

Figure 5.1. Urban Dibao's effects on reducing poverty rate in the general population (%). Note: $1 and $2 lines refer to the World Bank $1 and $2 per person per day purchasing power parity (PPP) poverty lines. Dibao line refers to the local city Dibao lines. Sources: Du and Park (2007), using the China Urban Labor Survey (CULS) data collected in five major cities (Shanghai, Wuhan, Shenyang, Fuzhou, and Xi'an).

day, Dibao reduced the poverty rate by only less than or close to one percentage point in 2001. This reduction was slightly larger in 2005, reaching about 1.5 percentage points, but remained a very small effect.

How effective has Dibao been at reducing poverty in its target population? Selection bias is an inherent challenge in evaluating the performance of targeting programs such as Dibao. Equally qualifying families may or may not choose to apply for the benefit, and even if they do apply, they may or may not be granted benefits. As shown in Chapter 4, leakage and mis-targeting are serious problems embedded not only in Dibao but also in every other means-tested cash transfer program around the world (Coady et al., 2004). These realities make the estimation of Dibao's anti-poverty effectiveness empirically challenging.

To at least partly address this challenge, my colleagues and I (Gao, Yang, et al., 2015) used a propensity score matching (PSM) method to match Dibao recipients with their non-recipient peers based on a rich array of family characteristics, so that the two groups were similar in not only their pre-Dibao household per capita income levels but also a variety of demographic and socioeconomic characteristics. We also controlled for city fixed effects, so that the heterogeneity in Dibao policies and other contextual factors across cities was accounted for. The matched households had very similar observed characteristics and thus could be conceptualized as belonging to the treatment (i.e., Dibao recipient) and control (i.e., non-Dibao recipient) groups. This approach, though not perfect in assessing Dibao's causal effects on reducing poverty, helped achieve a more accurate estimation of its anti-poverty effectiveness than otherwise possible (Dehejia & Wahba, 2002; Jalan & Ravallion, 2003; Rosenbaum & Rubin, 1983).

Using the China Household Income Project (CHIP) 2002 and 2007 urban survey data and the World Bank $1.25 and $2 per person per day PPP poverty lines, we compared the poverty rate, gap, and severity indices between the matched households within the eligible sample to estimate Dibao's anti-poverty effectiveness in its target population. We also estimated one counterfactual case in which recipients in the matched eligible sample lost their Dibao income. This aided us in understanding what Dibao had helped to achieve in reducing poverty among this group, especially in comparison to their matched non-recipient peers.

Table 5.2 presents poverty outcomes for the matched eligible sample using the World Bank $1.25 per person per day PPP poverty line estimated by Gao, Yang, and Li (2015). In the top panel, matched Dibao recipients and non-recipients are compared in terms of their poverty rate, gap, and severity indices. The matched Dibao recipients are considered the treatment group, and the matched non-recipients are considered the control group. The poverty reduction effect was calculated as the percentage of reduction in the respective poverty rate, gap, and severity outcomes—that is, the difference between poverty outcomes for Dibao recipients and non-recipients divided by the outcome for non-recipients, or the control group.

Table 5.2. Anti-Poverty Effectiveness of Urban Dibao among Matched Eligible Sample Using World Bank $1.25 per Person per Day PPP Poverty Line

	Poverty Rate		Poverty Gap		Poverty Severity	
	2002	2007	2002	2007	2002	2007
Matched Non-Recipients vs. Recipients						
Non-recipients	0.49	0.46	0.11	0.23	0.05	0.30
Recipients	0.38	0.18	0.09	0.07	0.04	0.05
Poverty reduction (%)	22%	61%	22%	69%	27%	83%
Recipients without vs. with Dibao Income						
Recipients without Dibao income	0.64	0.66	0.18	0.44	0.08	0.52
Recipients with Dibao income	0.38	0.18	0.09	0.07	0.04	0.05
Poverty reduction (%)	40%	73%	52%	84%	56%	90%

Source: Figure 5 in Gao, Yang, and Li (2015), using China Household Income Project (CHIP) 2002 and 2007 urban survey data. In the top panel, the poverty reduction effect was calculated as the difference between poverty outcomes for Dibao non-recipients and recipients divided by the outcome for non-recipients. In the bottom panel, the poverty reduction effect was calculated as the difference between poverty outcomes for Dibao recipients without and with Dibao income divided by the outcome without Dibao income.

The bottom panel presents the counterfactual case and compares the poverty outcomes among Dibao recipients with and without their Dibao income. The poverty reduction effects for the recipient group was then estimated by the percentage reduction in poverty outcomes due to Dibao income—that is, the difference between poverty outcomes for Dibao recipients with and without Dibao income divided by the outcome when they did not have Dibao income, or the counterfactual case.

Table 5.2 shows that Dibao reduced poverty in both 2002 and 2007, but the poverty reduction effects were much greater in 2007 than in 2002. In both years, the effects were greater for the poverty severity and poverty gap than for the poverty rate. A comparison of the matched recipients and non-recipients shows that Dibao lowered the poverty rate by 28 percentage points in 2007, a 61% reduction, as compared to a 16-percentage point, or 22%, reduction in 2002. The counterfactual analysis shows that, without the Dibao income, the poverty rate among recipients would have been 48 percentage points higher in 2007, suggesting a 73% poverty reduction effect among recipients, as compared to a 26-percentage point, or 40%, reduction in 2002.

The reductions in the poverty gap and severity due to Dibao were larger than those in the poverty rate in both years. They persisted over time and became larger in magnitude in 2007 than in 2002. As compared to their matched non-recipient peers, in 2007, Dibao reduced the poverty gap and severity among recipients by 69% and 83%, respectively—much larger effects than the 22% and 27% reductions in 2002. When compared to the counterfactual case where Dibao recipients lost their Dibao income, Dibao's anti-poverty effectiveness was even more pronounced. The poverty gap and severity were reduced by 84% and 90%, respectively, in 2007, larger than the 52% and 56% reductions observed in 2002. This suggests that, without Dibao, recipients could fall into much deeper and more severe poverty as compared to their non-recipient peers. This simulation exercise showed that Dibao indeed played a significant anti-poverty role for its recipients, especially when compared to their matched non-recipient peers.

My colleagues and I (Gao, Yang et al., 2015) also used the higher World Bank $2 per person per day PPP poverty line; the results are shown in Table 5.3. Dibao's anti-poverty effectiveness was smaller when this higher poverty line was used, as compared to the estimates based on the $1.25 line, but the overall result patterns remained consistent, with Dibao having larger anti-poverty effects in 2007 than in 2002 and playing a more influential role in reducing the poverty gap and severity than the poverty rate.

The second set of studies used a national poverty line to estimate Dibao's anti-poverty effectiveness in both urban and rural settings. Typically set up by the national government, a national poverty line is often used to gauge poverty within the unique national context, considering its economic development stage and historical trends. In China, the government has never set a national poverty line for urban areas, leaving researchers to define and estimate such a line when

Table 5.3. Anti-Poverty Effectiveness of Urban Dibao among Matched Eligible Sample Using World Bank $2 per Person per Day PPP Poverty Line

	Poverty Rate		Poverty Gap		Poverty Severity	
	2002	2007	2002	2007	2002	2007
Matched Non-Recipients vs. Recipients						
Non-recipients	0.96	0.82	0.36	0.39	0.17	0.30
Recipients	0.87	0.63	0.32	0.21	0.15	0.10
Poverty reduction (%)	9%	22%	9%	46%	13%	66%
Recipients without vs. with Dibao Income						
Recipients without Dibao income	0.96	0.83	0.43	0.57	0.23	0.52
Recipients with Dibao income	0.87	0.63	0.32	0.21	0.15	0.10
Poverty reduction (%)	9%	23%	24%	63%	36%	80%

Source: Figure 6 in Gao, Yang, and Li (2015), using China Household Income Project (CHIP) 2002 and 2007 urban survey data. In the top panel, the poverty reduction effect was calculated as the difference between poverty outcomes for Dibao non-recipients and recipients divided by the outcome for non-recipients. In the bottom panel, the poverty reduction effect was calculated as the difference between poverty outcomes for Dibao recipients without and with Dibao income divided by the outcome without Dibao income.

needed. The government set the national poverty line for rural areas at 1,196 yuan per person per year before 2011 and raised it to 2,300 yuan per person per year since 2011.

In order to assess Dibao's anti-poverty effectiveness in urban areas using a national poverty line, several studies have used a poverty line estimated by Khan (2004) according to the minimum food intake required to sustain energy (i.e., 2,100 kilocalories per person per day) in the Chinese context. This line was then adjusted by provincial price deflators estimated by Brandt and Holz (2006) and updated using provincial consumer price indices (CPIs) reported in the China Statistical Yearbooks (National Bureau of Statistics [NBS], 2005-2010a).

Using this poverty line and the CHIP 2002 urban data, as shown in Table 5.4, Gustafsson and Deng (2011) found that Dibao reduced the poverty rate by 16% among the recipients and by 5% among all urban households. More significantly, the poverty gap was narrowed by 29% among Dibao recipients and by 12% among all urban households, while poverty severity was reduced by 38% for Dibao recipients and by 20% for all urban households. These findings are consistent with those discussed earlier when the World Bank poverty lines are used.

Using the same poverty line, I estimated Dibao's anti-poverty effectiveness among a sample of 500 low-income families in a Shanghai community in 2009–2010 (Gao, 2013). The effect patterns identified in this study were consistent with those found by Gustafsson and Deng (2011), but the effect sizes were larger, possibly because of the study's focus on Dibao's target population and Shanghai's more generous Dibao transfers than those in other cities. Specifically, as shown in the top panel of Table 5.5, Dibao lowered the poverty rate in this sample of

Table 5.4. Anti-Poverty Effectiveness of the Urban Dibao among Recipients and the General Population in 2002 Using Khan (2004) Poverty Line

	Poverty Rate	Poverty Gap	Poverty Severity
Dibao Recipients			
Pre-Dibao	0.494	0.177	0.091
Post-Dibao	0.414	0.126	0.056
Poverty reduction (%)	16%	29%	38%
Non-recipients	0.046	0.011	0.005
All Households			
Pre-Dibao	0.063	0.017	0.008
Post-Dibao	0.060	0.015	0.007
Poverty reduction (%)	5%	12%	20%

Source: Table 6 in Gustafsson and Deng (2011), using China Household Income Project (CHIP) 2002 urban survey data. The Khan (2004) poverty line was estimated according to the minimum food intake required to sustain energy (i.e., 2,100 kilocalories per person per day). For both the Dibao recipients and all households, the poverty reduction effect was calculated as the difference between pre- and post-Dibao poverty outcomes divided by the pre-Dibao outcome.

Table 5.5. Anti-Poverty Effectiveness of Dibao among a Sample of 500 Low-Income Families in Shanghai, 2009–2010

	Poverty Rate	Poverty Gap	Poverty Severity
Khan (2004) Poverty Line			
Pre-Dibao	0.30	0.16	0.12
Post-Dibao	0.16	0.06	0.03
Poverty reduction (%)	47%	64%	78%
Relative Poverty Line set at 50% of Median City Income			
Pre-Dibao	0.97	0.59	0.42
Post-Dibao	0.95	0.51	0.32
Poverty reduction (%)	2%	12%	23%
Relative Poverty Line set at 25% of Median City Income			
Pre-Dibao	0.65	0.32	0.22
Post-Dibao	0.60	0.21	0.11
Poverty reduction (%)	7%	34%	50%

Source: Table 3 in Gao (2013), using data collected among a sample of 500 low-income families in a Shanghai community in 2009–2010. The Khan (2004) poverty line was estimated according to the minimum food intake required to sustain energy (i.e., 2,100 kilocalories per person per day). For each poverty line, the poverty reduction effect was calculated as the difference between pre- and post-Dibao poverty outcomes divided by the pre-Dibao outcome.

low-income families by 47%, and it reduced the poverty gap and severity by 64% and 78%, respectively.

In the case of rural Dibao, nearly all existing studies have used the national rural poverty line set by the Chinese government to assess Dibao's anti-poverty effectiveness. The findings are very consistent with the patterns identified for urban Dibao: Rural Dibao had greater anti-poverty effectiveness among Dibao recipients than among the general population, and it played a larger role in reducing the poverty gap and severity than it did in decreasing the poverty rate.

Deng and Li (2010) used the national rural poverty line of 1,196 yuan per person per year to estimate Dibao's anti-poverty effectiveness among Dibao recipients and the general population. They used data from the 2008 Rural Poverty Monitoring Survey collected by the NBS, which drew a sample of 53,270 households in 592 nationally designated poor counties. Seven percent of the sample, or 3,835 households, were Dibao recipients. This share was higher than the national average rural Dibao population coverage rate of 6%.

As shown in Table 5.6, among Dibao recipients, rural Dibao lowered the poverty rate by 21%, the poverty gap by 33%, and poverty severity by 38%, all substantial effects. However, rural Dibao's anti-poverty effects among the general population were much more limited, reducing the poverty rate, gap, and severity by only 2 to 4%, respectively. These effects were much smaller than the anti-poverty effects of urban Dibao among the general population that were estimated by Gustafsson and Deng (2011) and discussed earlier. This is partly because that the sample for this study was drawn from designated poor counties and thus was more disadvantaged than the broader rural population.

Table 5.6. Anti-Poverty Effectiveness of Rural Dibao among Recipients and the General Population in 2008 Using the National Poverty Line (1,196 yuan per person per year)

	Poverty Rate	**Poverty Gap**	**Poverty Severity**
Dibao Recipients			
Pre-Dibao	0.239	0.072	0.036
Post-Dibao	0.189	0.049	0.022
Poverty reduction (%)	21%	33%	38%
Non-recipients	0.143	0.044	0.041
All Households			
Pre-Dibao	0.150	0.046	0.040
Post-Dibao	0.147	0.045	0.039
Poverty reduction (%)	2%	4%	3%

Source: Deng and Li (2010), as reported in Table 9 in Li and Sicular (2014), using data from the 2008 Rural Poverty Monitoring Survey collected by the National Bureau of Statistics. For both Dibao recipients and all households, the poverty reduction effect was calculated as the difference between pre- and post-Dibao poverty outcomes divided by the pre-Dibao outcome.

Applying the new rural national poverty line of 2,300 yuan per person per year set in 2011, Golan et al. (2014) used the CHIP 2007–2009 rural survey data and found that rural Dibao had a somewhat greater effect against poverty in the general population than that identified by Deng and Li (2010). Because the CHIP 2007–2009 rural surveys did not ask about the exact amount of Dibao transfers received by families, the authors used county average amounts of Dibao transfer as an approximation at the household level. They found that rural Dibao narrowed the poverty gap by 2% in 2007, 3% in 2008, and 7% in 2009, suggesting that Dibao played a growing anti-poverty role in rural China during this period.

To compare the influence of the old and new national rural poverty lines (1,196 yuan vs. 2,300 yuan per person per year), Han and Xu (2014) used data collected from 9,107 rural households in five central and western provinces in 2010 and applied both poverty lines to examine rural Dibao's effects on reducing the poverty rate, gap, and severity. They estimated these effects among three samples: the Dibao recipient sample, the overall sample including all households, and the eligible sample. As expected and consistent with the urban result patterns, Dibao's poverty reduction effect was greater when the lower old national poverty line was used and smaller when the higher new national poverty line was used.

The authors found that rural Dibao's anti-poverty effectiveness was most prominent among the Dibao recipient sample, followed by the general population, and least for the eligible sample. This is because of the serious targeting error in rural Dibao, as identified by the authors in the same study and discussed in Chapter 4, resulting in many eligible families either not receiving any Dibao benefits or receiving only a proportion of their entitled amount of benefit. The mis-targeted families (i.e., those ineligible but receiving benefits) actually benefited more from Dibao transfers, which yielded a greater impact on poverty reduction in the general rural population than in the eligible sample.

Specifically, as shown in Table 5.7, using the old national rural poverty line of 1,196 yuan per person per year, Dibao lowered the poverty rate among its recipients by 36%, the poverty gap by 51%, and poverty severity by 61%. These reductions were smaller but still quite significant when the new national rural poverty line of 2,300 yuan per person per year was used: the reductions for poverty rate, gap, and severity among Dibao recipients were 16%, 30%, and 40%, respectively. Consistent with the findings in urban areas, Dibao had the largest effect on reducing poverty severity, followed by the poverty gap and then poverty rate.

Among the general population, rural Dibao's anti-poverty effectiveness was much more limited, consistent with the finding in the urban Dibao literature. Using the old national rural poverty line, Dibao lowered the poverty rate in the general population by 9%, the poverty gap by 16%, and poverty severity by 20%. When the new poverty line was used, these reductions were even smaller: 3%, 8%, and 11%, respectively.

Table 5.7. Anti-Poverty Effectiveness of Rural Dibao among Recipients, the General Population, and Eligible Families in 2010 Using Old and New National Poverty Lines (1,196 yuan and 2,300 yuan per person per year)

National Poverty Line	Poverty Rate		Poverty Gap		Poverty Severity	
	Old	New	Old	New	Old	New
Dibao Recipients						
Pre-Dibao	0.285	0.541	0.131	0.258	0.083	0.166
Post-Dibao	0.183	0.456	0.064	0.182	0.032	0.099
Poverty reduction (%)	36%	16%	51%	30%	61%	40%
All Households						
Pre-Dibao	0.104	0.237	0.042	0.099	0.024	0.059
Post-Dibao	0.094	0.229	0.035	0.092	0.019	0.052
Poverty reduction (%)	9%	3%	16%	8%	20%	11%
Eligible Households						
Pre-Dibao	0.988	1.000	0.455	0.704	0.275	0.516
Post-Dibao	0.930	0.999	0.396	0.665	0.227	0.468
Poverty reduction (%)	6%	0%	13%	5%	18%	9%

Source: Tables 2–4 in Han and Xu (2014), using data collected among 9,107 rural households in five provinces (Jiangxi, Anhui, Henan, Shaanxi, and Gansu) in central and western China in 2010. The poverty reduction effects were calculated as the difference between pre- and post-Dibao poverty outcomes divided by the pre-Dibao outcome.

As noted earlier, the authors of this study found that Dibao's impact on reducing poverty among its eligible population (i.e., those whose pre-Dibao family income was below the local Dibao lines) was even smaller than that among the general population, most notably due to the serious targeting errors identified in rural Dibao, as demonstrated in Figure 4.4 in Chapter 4. Using the old national rural poverty line, Dibao reduced the poverty rate, gap, and severity among the eligible population by 6%, 13%, and 18%, respectively. When the higher new poverty line was used, Dibao had negligible impact on reducing the poverty rate. The poverty gap and severity among the eligible sample were respectively lowered by 5% and 9%, reductions that were much smaller than those among Dibao recipients and the general population.

The third set of studies used the local Dibao line as the poverty line to estimate urban Dibao's anti-poverty effectiveness. Because the Dibao lines vary to a great extent across localities, the estimated poverty reduction effects of Dibao also vary according to the cities included in the samples. In rural areas, however, no existing studies have used local Dibao lines as the poverty line to investigate Dibao's anti-poverty effectiveness.

As shown in Table 5.8, using the Urban Household Short Survey (UHSS) 2003–2004 data collected from 76,000 households in China's 35 largest cities

Table 5.8. Anti-Poverty Effectiveness of Urban Dibao among Recipients and the General Population, 2003–2004, Using Local Dibao Lines as Poverty Line

	Poverty Rate	Poverty Gap	Poverty Severity
Dibao Recipients			
Pre-Dibao	0.569	0.199	0.102
Post-Dibao	0.455	0.142	0.064
Poverty reduction (%)	20%	29%	37%
All Households			
Pre-Dibao	0.077	0.023	0.010
Post-Dibao	0.073	0.021	0.009
Poverty reduction (%)	5%	9%	10%

Source: Table 2 in Chen, Ravallion, and Wang (2006), using Urban Household Short Survey (UHSS) collected in the 35 largest cities. For both the Dibao recipients and all households, the poverty reduction effect was calculated as the difference between pre- and post-Dibao poverty outcomes divided by the pre-Dibao outcome.

and the city Dibao lines as the poverty line, Chen et al. (2006) found that, for recipients, Dibao lowered the poverty rate by 20%, the poverty gap by 29%, and poverty severity by 37%. For all urban households, the reductions were much smaller at 5%, 9%, and 10%, respectively. The magnitudes of these poverty reduction effects were similar to those identified by Gustafsson and Deng (2011) using the CHIP 2002 data and the Khan (2004) poverty line, as the mean of the city Dibao lines used in this study (2,715 yuan per person per year in 2003) was very close to the Khan (2004) poverty line (2,534 yuan per person per year in 2002) in value.

Using the CHIP 2007 urban survey data collected in 91 cities from 16 provinces, Li and Yang (2009) treated provincial average Dibao lines as the poverty line to estimate Dibao's poverty reduction effects on the urban population as a whole. They found that Dibao lowered the poverty rate by 42%, poverty gap by 56%, and poverty severity by 63%, and the poverty reduction effects were larger in the central and western provinces than in the eastern provinces. Because the provincial average Dibao lines were much lower than the Dibao lines of the 35 largest cities, the poverty reduction results seem to be more promising based on this study than in the Chen et al. (2006) study. However, it is important to point out that, even when the very low provincial average Dibao lines are used as the poverty line, the urban poverty rate was not even halved, and Dibao was still far from eliminating poverty. This study also found that Dibao was only able to reduce income inequality as measured by the Gini coefficient and Theil index to a very small extent.

The last set of studies adopted relative poverty lines set relative to the median household income in society to gauge Dibao's anti-poverty effectiveness, taking into consideration the overall income distribution in the society. As the relative poverty lines are typically set at 50% or 60% of median income, which tends to be much higher than all of the three types of poverty lines discussed earlier, these researchers found that Dibao's anti-poverty effectiveness is much more limited when a relative poverty line is used than when any of the previously discussed absolute poverty lines are used.

Specifically, using the CHIP 2002 urban survey data, my colleagues and I (Gao, Garfinkel, et al., 2009) adopted a relative poverty line defined as 50% of national urban median income and found that Dibao reduced the poverty rate by only 2%, the poverty gap by 14%, and poverty severity by 26%. Using a poverty line set at 50% of median city income, I (Gao, 2013) estimated Dibao's anti-poverty effectiveness among a sample of 500 low-income families in a Shanghai community in 2009–2010. I found that Dibao lowered the poverty rate by 2%, the poverty gap by 12%, and poverty severity by 23%, as shown in Table 5.5. These reductions were much smaller than those identified in the same study when the Khan (2004) absolute poverty line was used. Revising the relative poverty line to 25% of median city income, I found somewhat larger poverty reduction effects from Dibao; it reduced the poverty rate, gap, and severity by 2%, 34%, and 50% respectively. These effects, however, were still much smaller than when the absolute poverty line was used.

Using the China Health and Nutrition Survey (CHNS) 1989 and 2009 data, Lu and colleagues (Lu, Lin, Vikse, & Huang, 2013) also adopted a relative poverty line set at 50% of national urban median income and discovered very limited poverty reduction effects from social assistance transfers. These transfers included subsidies to low-income families and disabled persons, and by 2009, the majority of these transfers were from Dibao. The authors found that, in both years, social assistance transfers lowered the poverty rate and narrowed income inequality gap by only less than one percentage point, a very small effect.

In sum, evidence based on the various poverty lines and across urban and rural areas suggests that Dibao's effectiveness in alleviating poverty is limited and at best modest, largely due to its targeting errors and benefit delivery gaps (Umapathi et al., 2013). Dibao was more effective in reducing poverty severity and gap than the poverty rate, and its anti-poverty effectiveness was greater among recipients than in the general population. There is some evidence that rural Dibao had smaller poverty reduction effects among the eligible population than in the general population, mainly due to the serious population and benefit targeting errors in rural Dibao (Han & Xu, 2014). Dibao's impact on poverty reduction is larger when a lower poverty line is used and smaller when a higher poverty line is used. This partially explains its very small anti-poverty effects when relative poverty lines are used, as these lines are typically set relative to the median income in society and tend to be much higher than the more widely used absolute poverty lines.

FACTORS INFLUENCING DIBAO'S ANTI-POVERTY EFFECTIVENESS

Given the modest anti-poverty effectiveness of Dibao based on different poverty lines, what are some deterrents of and contributors to Dibao's poverty reduction effects? What can be done in the future to improve Dibao's anti-poverty performance? A set of quantitative and qualitative studies has identified the key deterrents and contributors at both the household and policy levels.

First and foremost, at the household level, some demographic characteristics continue to serve as barriers to Dibao's poverty reduction effects. Using the CHNS data collected in 1993, 1997, 2000, 2004, 2006, and 2009 from about 4,400 households in nine provinces, Wu and Ramesh (2014) identified a set of such characteristics that make certain families more vulnerable than others in the urban setting. These include low education, lack of employment skills, lack of formal employment, and large household size, especially those with more children. These factors are mostly the same as those associated with a higher likelihood of becoming a Dibao recipient and receiving more benefits, as discussed in Chapter 4, yet they remain strong predictors of staying in poverty despite receiving Dibao support. This finding highlights the additional disadvantages faced by these families, as well as the challenges for Dibao to help them rise above poverty.

Second, at the policy level, several key elements of Dibao's design and implementation have important influence on its anti-poverty effectiveness. These include Dibao generosity, targeting performance, benefit delivery, and population coverage. In particular, more generous Dibao benefits, better targeting, fuller benefit delivery, and broader population coverage all lead to greater anti-poverty effectiveness of Dibao. These factors are influential for both urban and rural Dibao.

In the case of urban Dibao, using a hierarchical linear modeling (HLM) approach to further investigate the possible influence of Dibao policy on its anti-poverty effectiveness, Wu and Ramesh (2014) found that the generosity of Dibao spending played a crucial role in its poverty reduction effects. The more generous the Dibao spending, the greater its anti-poverty effectiveness. Using the World Bank $1 per person per day PPP poverty line, the authors found that both the government's total spending on Dibao as a percentage of provincial GDP and the provincial per capita Dibao expenditure level had significant positive effects on poverty reduction. These results were robust after taking into consideration the level of economic development and population size of the provinces. This finding highlights the importance of benefit generosity in helping to amplify Dibao's anti-poverty effectiveness.

In the case of rural Dibao, Deng and Li (2010) conducted county-level analysis using data from the 2008 Rural Poverty Monitoring Survey collected in 592 nationally designated poor counties. They found that Dibao generosity, as measured by the county average rural Dibao line, and its population coverage were both positively associated with reductions in poverty rate, gap, and severity. Dibao's leakage rate was found to have a negative impact on its anti-poverty effectiveness, especially on reducing poverty gap and severity. Dibao's mis-targeting rate, however, was found to have no significant impact on its anti-poverty performance, suggesting that many of these "mis-targeted" families in fact had similar pre-Dibao income levels to those of families who were the intended target population, and the inclusion of them resulted in no additional costs or benefits to poverty reduction. Han and Xu (2014) conducted township-level analysis using data collected in 90 townships across 5 provinces in central and western China in 2010 and achieved very similar findings.

SUMMARY AND IMPLICATIONS

Based on a thorough review of the existing evidence, this chapter offers an assessment of Dibao's anti-poverty effectiveness and highlights the factors that influence Dibao's anti-poverty performance. To begin with, Dibao families have lower household income and fewer assets than their non-Dibao peers. Dibao is the main income source for most recipient families. Their Dibao income is supplemented by other sources that are often irregular and in the form of odd jobs or support from friends and relatives.

Estimates based on various poverty lines and across urban and rural areas show that Dibao's anti-poverty effectiveness is limited and at best modest, largely due to its inadequate benefits as well as targeting errors and gaps in benefit delivery. Dibao was more effective in reducing poverty depth and severity than the poverty rate, and its anti-poverty effectiveness was greater among recipients than in the general population. Dibao's influence on reducing poverty is greater when a lower poverty line is used and smaller when a higher poverty line is used. Because relative poverty lines are often set relative to the median income in society and tend to be much higher than the more widely used absolute poverty lines, Dibao's effects on reducing relative poverty are especially limited. Dibao also had a very limited effect on reducing income inequality in society.

Certain individual and household characteristics as well as policy factors have a particularly significant impact on Dibao's anti-poverty effectiveness. At the household level, individuals and families with low education, low employment skills, informal or no employment, and large household size, especially those with more children, are more likely to be poor even after accounting for Dibao support. At the policy level, more generous Dibao benefits, better targeting, more effective benefit delivery, and broader population coverage all lead to greater anti-poverty effectiveness of Dibao.

These findings offer important policy implications. First and foremost, despite the poverty reductions achieved by Dibao observed in multiple studies, it is evident that Dibao is still far from eliminating poverty, even when the local Dibao line is used as the poverty threshold. This suggests that Dibao is an insufficient last resort for poor families and needs to be strengthened in its design and implementation to improve its anti-poverty effectiveness. Key to this improvement is increasing the amount of Dibao benefits and population coverage, both of which contribute substantially to greater reductions in poverty. Better targeting, especially decreasing the leakage rate, would also be helpful.

In particular, Dibao generosity can be addressed locally with the support of the central government, given the decentralized nature of Dibao implementation. Evidence from this and earlier chapters suggests that greater financial commitment from both the local and central governments is one of the strongest and most robust predictors of improved targeting and anti-poverty performance of Dibao. For the localities that can afford it, having a more generous Dibao program would definitely help with outcomes of poverty alleviation. For the localities that have limited financial resources, especially those from the western and central regions, greater support from the central government is needed in order to reduce poverty and narrow the persistent gaps in living standards across regions and localities.

Second, these findings highlight the existence of a broader poor and near-poor group that is not always targeted by Dibao. While the families who are erroneously excluded from Dibao are indeed poor and need to be covered, mistargeted families are also poor and need support from Dibao or other public assistance programs. In addition, families who are neither excluded nor mistargeted but nonetheless live below or just above the various poverty lines also need to be considered. Out of the reach of Dibao and its supplementary programs, this group might be particularly invisible to policymakers and the public and suffer from multiple vulnerabilities. To achieve the broader anti-poverty goal of living beyond the bare minimum of survival, the broader poor and near-poor populations should be included in future policy discussions.

Third, the existing research on Dibao's anti-poverty effectiveness overwhelmingly relies on income measures. While this is very valuable and offers important policy lessons, other measures that more accurately capture family consumption needs and patterns, material deprivation and hardship, and subjective well-being need to be considered in future research and policy discussions. Relying solely on income measures may be one of the key reasons for Dibao's targeting errors and limited poverty reduction effects. For poor families, these additional dimensions often better reflect their actual living conditions than does income. More research evidence needs to be provided on these outcome dimensions to better inform Dibao's policy design and incorporate them into future reforms.

6

FROM WELFARE TO WORK

Like many other social assistance programs around the world, the goal of Dibao is to provide a basic safety net for the poor, but it could also function as a trap for welfare dependency and a deterrent rather than stimulus for recipients' work efforts. Dibao may deter work activities implicitly because any earned income would be counted toward household income, which may disqualify these families from receiving Dibao. In the Chinese context, this disincentive might be especially strong, as eligibility for supplementary social assistance for education, health, and housing are closely tied to Dibao eligibility. In other words, becoming eligible for Dibao opens the door for recipients to gain access to these other benefits, which often trump Dibao benefits in value and helpfulness for recipients' lives, while leaving Dibao means instantly becoming ineligible for these other important benefits. This tied eligibility rule prescribed by the current system offers a strong disincentive for Dibao recipients to move off the welfare roll.

In this chapter, I first describe the extent of work activities and welfare dependency among Dibao recipients. I further examine the various barriers to Dibao recipients' work efforts at the individual, family, community, and policy levels, drawing on multiple empirical studies. Next I review local government initiatives to stimulate and support the transition from welfare to work and provide an assessment of their effectiveness where evidence is available. I conclude this chapter by discussing policy implications and proposing future directions for addressing welfare dependency and promoting work efforts among Dibao's target population.

WORK ACTIVITIES AND WELFARE DEPENDENCY AMONG DIBAO RECIPIENTS

Over half of Dibao recipients are working-age adults. Do they work? What kind of jobs do they hold? And, if they do not work, do they actively seek employment? After finding employment, are they able to maintain a job? To what extent do they rely on welfare rather than strive to move from welfare to work? What role does stigma play? Is it such a strong and lasting social label that Dibao recipients become used to and identified with welfare and are reluctant to pursue work, or does it carry such profound stigma that Dibao recipients do their best to leave welfare and free themselves of such a label?

An evaluation project commissioned by the Asian Development Bank (ADB) offers unique insights into the plight of Dibao families, based on household survey data in three cities (Baotou, Changsha, and Jinan) in 2012 (Xu, 2013). Overall, 93% of the 2,810 Dibao households in the sample had family members with ability to work. Consistent with the national picture shown in Figure 3.8 in Chapter 3, among the 2,550 working-age respondents (aged 20–55 years) in the sample who reported employment information, 59% were working—including 7% who were formally employed and 52% with informal jobs—and 41% were unemployed. It is reasonable to assume that those who did not report their employment status tended to be unemployed or employed informally.

There were also significant variations across the three cities among these working-age respondents: The western city of Baotou, the least developed of the three cities, had the lowest formal employment rate (3.5%) and the highest informal employment rate (67%), with an unemployment rate of 29%. The eastern city of Jinan, the most developed of the three cities, had the highest formal employment rate (11%). Its informal employment rate was 53%, lower than that of Baotou but higher than that of Changsha in the central region (38%), while its unemployment rate (36%) was higher than that of Baotou but lower than that of Changsha (55%). Indeed, Changsha's unemployment rate in this sample was alarmingly high (55%), highlighting the unique challenges faced by cities in central China where both local financial capacity and central government subsidy for Dibao have been lacking.

What kinds of jobs do Dibao recipients hold if they work? There are no official accounts regarding the nature of their jobs, but various ethnographic studies offer insights. Solinger (2012) observed that much of the occasional and part-time work performed by Dibao recipients in Wuhan and other cities of Hubei province was more in the nature of make-work rather than productive labor. Such jobs included "handing out leaflets on the streets; monitoring parking and pedestrian traffic along the sidewalks, tearing down ads and notices stuck to public walls in the communities; moving things; taking others' children to school; keeping track of births or other 'security'-related statistics for the community;

standing erect at gateway entrances in neighborhoods or at government offices; sweeping streets or pavings; and maintaining community green spaces" (Solinger, 2012, p. 1021). Through fieldwork in Shanghai in 2013, Solinger and Jiang (2016) found that there was a concerted effort to arrange training or work for Dibao recipients. They observed that local government officials created temporary jobs for the poor, such as assisting the police, helping urban management officials, or serving as underlings for social workers.

These menial jobs paid little but sometimes were sufficient to get recipients off the Dibao rolls, effectively removing their Dibao eligibility without increasing their income. These jobs, though not always requiring hard labor or much engagement, take the Dibao recipients away from taking care of household chores or family members. It is therefore no surprise that nearly 30% of working Dibao recipients were unsatisfied with their jobs and another 50% considered their jobs "so-so" in a community survey in Shanghai in 2009–2010 (Gao, 2015). Solinger's fieldwork also suggests that many Dibao recipients have to rely on additional income sources such as pensions, assets left by deceased parents (mainly housing that can be rented out to supplement livelihood), and support from grown children and other relatives (Solinger, 2015a).

Despite the work activities engaged in by many Dibao recipients and the job-seeking efforts of unemployed Dibao recipients, welfare dependency, or staying on welfare for a relatively long time, has been a common phenomenon. Based on the 2012 survey data from Baotou, Changsha, and Jinan, the average length of receiving Dibao for families in the sample was 5.4 years. As shown in Figure 6.1, 8% of all households in the sample had been receiving Dibao for over 10 years. Nearly one third of these households had been on welfare for 6 to 10 years, and

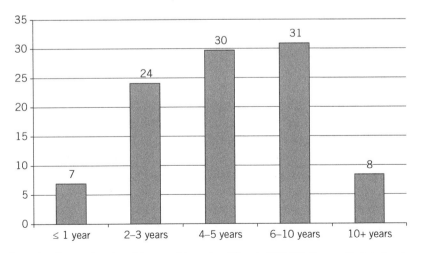

Figure 6.1. Average lengths of time receiving urban Dibao in 2012 (%). Source: Xu (2013), using data collected from 2,810 Dibao families in three cities (Jinan, Changsha, and Baotou).

about 30% for 4 to 5 years. Another quarter had been receiving Dibao for 2 to 3 years (Xu, 2013).

In a survey conducted among 1,209 Dibao recipients in six cities in 2007, Han and Guo (2012) found that most respondents started receiving Dibao in 1999, when the program was launched nationally in urban areas. On average, these respondents had been on welfare for 42.1 months, or 3.5 years. Based on their qualitative interviews, the authors found that most Dibao recipients relied on Dibao benefits to maintain their basic livelihood and still had strong motivation for seeking work. The authors also found, however, that the higher the Dibao benefits received by a family, the less likely its members would look for jobs.

BARRIERS TO MOVING FROM WELFARE TO WORK

What has led to such welfare dependency, given the high aspiration to find employment and the willingness to work hard in order to move from welfare to work? What factors facilitate moving from welfare to work? The barriers and facilitating factors, summarized in Table 6.1, are discussed next in detail. The main barriers for Dibao recipients to finding stable jobs and moving from welfare to work include their limited employability for various reasons; family care responsibilities; lack of community resources; and policy design factors.

Limited Employability: Poor Health, Low Education, and Lack of Social Capital

At the individual level, Dibao recipients often have limited employability due to poor health, chronic illness, low education, lack of skills, middle age, long history of unemployment, and lack of financial or social capital. These barriers hold for both urban and rural areas and are especially prominent for women and those suffering from health problems.

Poor health is the most widely cited reason for people to initially fall into poverty and then rely on welfare. It also serves as the most significant barrier for families to finding employment and leaving welfare. The most notable challenges related to poor health are disability and chronic illness. Nationally, in 2014, 8% of urban Dibao recipients and 9% of rural Dibao recipients were disabled (Ministry of Civil Affairs [MCA], 2015a). Among the 2,810 Dibao households surveyed in Baotou, Changsha, and Jinan in 2012, 74% reported having at least one member with chronic illness and 30% had at least one member with disability. These proportions were mostly consistent across the three cities: the share of families with chronically ill members ranged between 70% and 79%, and the share of families with disabled members ranged between 25% and 40% (Xu, 2013). Among the 1,209 Dibao recipients surveyed in 2007 in six cities, 19% had no work ability and 40% had only partial work ability due to disability or chronic illness (Han & Guo, 2012).

Table 6.1. Barriers to Moving from Welfare to Work

Individual level	Limited employability due to poor health, chronic illness, low levels of education, lack of skills, middle age, long history of unemployment, and lack of financial or social capital
Household level	Family care responsibilities, including caring for sick or disabled family members, childcare, elder care, and supporting child education
Community level	Lack of childcare and senior care services and facilities in the community, stigma from neighbors, and scrutiny from local Dibao officials
Policy level	Additional income as marginal taxes; restrictions on asset ownership and on lifestyle choices that limit upward mobility; tied eligibility for Dibao and other social assistance programs; and restrictions placed on Dibao recipients to "stay off the streets" and not set up small businesses or engage in activities that might disrupt "normal" economic activities or make streets look untidy

Through over 7 years of fieldwork and interviews with over 100 Dibao recipient families in eight cities, Solinger encountered plenty of Dibao families suffering from and struggling with disability and chronic illness. For example, in 2009, in Jingzhou of Hubei province, she met an elderly blind couple living in "dingy, ill-kept rooms with concrete floors." Another couple she met lived in "a kind of one-room loft whose space was mostly filled by one bed on which lay a paralyzed, mute woman and in which empty wine bottles littered the floor beneath a wooden dining table across from the bed, where sat an unhappy husband" (Solinger, 2012, p. 1020). Not explicitly acknowledged but vividly shown as an important part of this story is the drinking problem associated with despair faced by many Dibao families, which in turn worsens their financial as well as emotional state.

Many researchers studying Dibao have shed new light on the hidden problem of mental health in China. In both pre- and post-Communist China, mental health has been mostly hidden from the public and received little attention or policy intervention. However, researchers have discovered that many Dibao recipients suffer from mental illness, limiting their ability to seek employment or hold a job, while requiring family members to be dedicated caregivers.

Solinger has met many Dibao families struggling with mental illness in her fieldwork. For example, in Guangzhou in 2010, she interviewed a 56-year-old man who had lost the sight in his right eye and could not find any feasible job because he had to take care of his mentally ill wife. Solinger also met a laid-off 45-year-old woman who had to stay home nearly all the time to take care of her 22-year-old son with mental illness. Solinger quoted her as saying,

I can't leave my son; he can't do anything. I have to feed him three meals a day; if he were to boil some hot water I fear he'd get scalded. He's completely without intelligence; if he sees something he'll want to go play, like with those electrical plugs. I don't dare to get away; something could bring disaster to other people. (Solinger, 2012, pp. 1022–1023)

Adding to the health challenges faced by many Dibao recipients are their limited employability due to low level of education, lack of skills, middle age, and long history of unemployment. One participant of a 2007 in-depth interview in Beijing, conducted by a team of researchers from Renmin University of China, said,

How many jobs have I applied for? But no one wants me. No business wants me. (They would say) even though your skills are good, you are too old, so we cannot hire you. . . . I began learning skills right after graduating from school. . . . Now that I have skills, I cannot even feed myself. (Han 2012, p. 30).

(The interviewee was the husband of 54-year-old Ms. Ma, who was a Dibao recipient. Her husband had been unemployed for 7 years but did not want to apply for Dibao out of shame.)

The same challenge holds for rural Dibao recipients. Through focus groups in Baotou, Changsha, and Jinan in 2012, Xu (2013) found that many working-age rural Dibao recipients attributed their difficulty in finding a suitable job to their lack of education or skills required for the potential jobs.

Many of the Dibao recipients facing reemployment challenges simply cannot find a job because of their age. Most are in their 40s and 50s, which, unfortunately, in the current Chinese context is considered too old and unsuitable for many jobs. Among the 2,810 Dibao recipients surveyed in three cities in 2012, over half were between the ages 45 and 54 and another 40% were aged 34 to 45 (Xu, 2013). In a survey of 437 Dibao recipients in Shanghai in 2009–2010, the average age was 49 years, with 40% between ages 40 and 49 and 31% between ages 50 and 59 (Gao, 2013).

One Shanghai Dibao recipient interviewed by Chen and colleagues (2013) during 2009–2011 summarized these barriers vividly and concisely:

Age and education level [are my barriers to re-employment]. Many companies set up age requirements in the economic reform period, and then I was always excluded. Moreover, I was persecuted during the Cultural Revolution and my education level is poor. . . . I had no chance to study because I had to work shift duties at that time. (Chen, Wong, Zeng, & Hämäläinen, 2013, p. 333)

Employment opportunities for female Dibao recipients are especially rare as compared to their male counterparts. After accounting for various individual and policy factors, Han and Guo (2012) found that, among the sample with work ability, female Dibao recipients had a 7% lower probability of gaining employment than their male peers. When the sample was further restricted to those with full work ability, female Dibao recipients had a 14% lower chance of finding a job than their male peers.

Part of the reason for this discrepancy is that, compared to men, women lack social networks, a form of social capital and arguably the most important channel for finding work among low-income individuals in China. Through rich life history interviews and focus groups, Liu (2011) found that women in China bore the cost of economic restructuring disproportionately and were discriminated against by the labor market, society, and even social policies. To begin with, women were often made "redundant workers" (p. 82) involuntarily, sometimes through unnecessary extended maternity leaves. Women were not only responsible for caring for older parents and young children but also often treated as a labor reserve for care of family and extended kin, excluding them from the labor market for long periods of time or even permanently. Women in this study also shared their difficulty in re-entering the job market because of their lack of social networks, which play a crucial role in helping people land jobs, especially in the limited, tough job market faced by Dibao recipients.

In addition to lack of education, skills, and social networks, many Dibao recipients also have a long history of unemployment, which further distances them from social connections and any formal or informal job market. In the increasingly competitive labor market in China, the longer one stays out of the labor market, the harder it becomes to re-enter it. This reality is more poignant and alarming among Dibao recipients than their non-poor, higher-educated peers. Among the working-age Dibao recipients surveyed in three cities in 2012 (Xu, 2013), over two thirds of those currently employed had been unemployed for 5 years or longer. Those who were currently unemployed had even longer histories of unemployment: nearly one third had been unemployed for 15 years or more, another 30% for 10 to 15 years, and a quarter for 5 to 10 years.

All of these individual-level barriers join forces and deter Dibao recipients from seeking employment or keeping stable jobs. As summarized by one neighborhood official in Guangzhou interviewed by Solinger (2012, p. 1020), "The biggest issues facing the *dibaohu* (Dibao families) are illness and employment; since their age is rather old, their cultural (educational) level fairly low, it's hard for them to find appropriate work."

Family Care Responsibilities and Lack of Community Resources

At the household level, poor health of individual family members typically leads to family care responsibilities, another important welfare-to-work barrier. This challenge often adds to child and elder care responsibilities, especially when there are no child or elder care services and facilities in the community and when older members of the family have no pension. Dibao families also struggle to pay for their children's education with limited economic resources.

In the 2012 survey in three cities, nearly 55% of Dibao families reported having to take care of a child, elder, or disabled person, sometimes all simultaneously. Women were overwhelmingly identified as the main caregivers of children (76%) and of elders or family members with a disability (64%) (Xu, 2013).

Dibao recipients are well aware of these responsibilities and constraints when they try to move from welfare to work. Nearly two thirds of respondents in the same study identified proximity to home and convenience in caring for family members as one of the most important factors to consider when looking for a job. Among those who did not look for a job, about one third cited caring for dependent family members as their reason. In rural areas, sometimes Dibao recipients were forbidden from working in their own fields because they had family care responsibilities, making them depend on welfare even more (Xu, 2013).

This situation is coupled with a lack of community services providing care for the elderly, young children, or disabled and is echoed by many Dibao recipients through interviews and focus groups. Based on data gathered through focus groups, Xu (2013) recommended establishing dedicated service agencies in communities to provide free or low-fee services for Dibao recipients. Full-fee services could be provided for non-Dibao recipients so that the services would be financially sustainable. Indeed, ADB, in collaboration with MCA, has commissioned a demonstration project to investigate how social services might be integrated with social assistance most effectively. Early findings from this project suggest that professional social workers and social service agencies have certain advantages in identifying the needs of their target population more accurately and offering appropriate and timely services in response.

In addition, stigma from neighbors and scrutiny from local officers associated with the Dibao screening and approval process provide disincentives for Dibao recipients to move from welfare to work. Through in-depth interviews, many Dibao recipients cited examples of themselves or other Dibao recipients who had received harsh criticism and remarks questioning their Dibao eligibility if they engaged in work activities and seemed to bring home extra income. As a result, some Dibao recipients maintained that they would rather stay home and be idle or only engage in voluntary community work in order to avoid such criticism and the possibility of losing their Dibao eligibility (Han, 2012).

At the same time, the stigma associated with receiving Dibao sometimes plays a stimulus role in pushing able-bodied recipients to seek employment and exit welfare. Through regression models accounting for various individual characteristics, Han and Guo (2012) revealed that unwillingness to have one's name publicly displayed in the neighborhood was significantly associated with increased likelihood of working. This, however, was only true for those with work ability; it did not hold for those with only partial or no work ability.

Policy Design Barriers: Additional Income at 100% Marginal Tax Rate, Restrictions on Asset Ownership, Tied Eligibility for Social Assistance, and "Stay Off the Streets"

There are several policy barriers that are either inherent in Dibao's design or are closely tied to broader social assistance or employment policies. These include Dibao's means-testing nature, which by design treats any additional income at 100% marginal tax rate and could threaten Dibao eligibility; some local restrictions on ownership of certain assets such as computers or cell phones, which further limit Dibao recipients' ability to have social interactions and look for jobs; the reality that eligibility for other social assistance programs such as medical, education, housing, and temporary assistance often depends on eligibility for Dibao; and some local governments' efforts to keep Dibao recipients "off the streets" so as to keep streets tidy and maintain social order.

First, as a strictly means-testing program, Dibao by design treats any additional income earned or provided by friends and relatives at a 100% marginal tax rate, which immediately threatens benefit eligibility. Any additional income earned by family members will therefore offset the Dibao benefits they are entitled to. Among these additional income sources, income earned through work is often more visible and subject to closer monitoring and scrutiny. This provides a direct disincentive for Dibao recipients to obtain work. Han and Guo (2012) found that the higher the Dibao benefits received by a family, the less motivated its members were to seek jobs. This is an old dilemma faced by similar means-tested safety net programs in both developing and developed countries around the world (Eardley, Bradshaw, Ditch, Gough, & Whiteford, 1996; Grosh et al., 2008).

Most Dibao recipients who work have only informal and irregular jobs and thus are unable to fully rely on such income sources for escaping poverty. The determination of Dibao eligibility, however, is often based on one's monthly income, rather than taking into consideration the fluctuations in income experienced by many poor people who work odd jobs or in small businesses (e.g., street stalls). Therefore, Dibao recipients are worried that they will lose eligibility for the subsidy when they have some earned income but will not be able to regain their eligibility when work or income is no longer available (Solinger, 2009).

In addition, some local governments require able-bodied Dibao recipients to participate in "voluntary obligatory work," partly to prevent underground employment (Solinger, 2009, p. 322). These jobs often do not require many skills, nor do they provide any meaningful products. But they take time and motivation away from recipients for real job searches and limit their chances of being successful in the labor market.

Indeed, Dibao recipients have expressed their wishes that the 100% marginal tax rate associated with any additional income be removed or reduced. In their survey of 1,209 Dibao recipients in six cities in 2007, Han and Guo (2012) found that 9.5% of respondents wished that only part of their earnings from employment would be counted toward family income when Dibao officials carried out means testing. Nearly a quarter (22.7%) wanted their Dibao eligibility to be maintained for another 2 to 3 months even after they found a job to earn income.

Recognizing these realities, many local Dibao officials do not regard any income gain as stable income that would be immediately considered in assessing Dibao eligibility. They tend to use multiple approaches to discount the 100% marginal tax rate, to avoid engendering a strong work disincentive. For example, some local officials delay withdrawal of benefits when a Dibao recipient gets a new job, until the job situation becomes stabilized. Others include only a proportion of the additional income for means-testing purposes (O'Keefe, 2004; Xu, 2013). These local measures aim to support welfare-to-work transitions without fundamentally modifying the means-testing nature of the Dibao program.

Constrained by the lack of longitudinal data for analyzing the actual work effort response to the 100% marginal tax rate from Dibao recipients, using the Urban Household Short Survey (UHSS) 2003–2004 data collected in China's 35 largest cities, Chen, Ravallion, and Wang (2006) used OLS and tobit regressions as well as instrumental variable techniques to estimate the benefit withdrawal rate. In other words, for beneficiaries, to what extent does receiving Dibao provide a disincentive to work? Their calculations yielded a benefit withdrawal rate ranging from −0.001 to −0.004, all statistically significant but very low in value. This suggests that the marginal tax rate for any additional income gained through work is very small, even after considering measurement errors in income. The authors thus argued that Dibao was unlikely to provide any serious disincentive for earning income through work, a finding that warrants further investigation using longitudinal data and fieldwork. The authors also conceded that part of the reason for this low estimated benefit withdrawal rate could be that Dibao was not really reaching the poorest individuals and those most in need because of its targeting errors, discussed in Chapter 4. For these individuals, the marginal tax rate on additional income would be higher. Ravallion and Chen (2015) used the 2007 UHSS data to update these results and reached similar conclusions. The estimated benefit withdrawal rate ranged from −0.03 to −0.14, which is larger than rates estimated based on the 2003–2004 data, but still small in magnitude and much lower than the supposed 100% marginal tax rate according to the policy design.

The second policy design discouraging a transition from welfare to work is that many localities have rules against Dibao recipients owning certain assets such as computers, phones, and motorized vehicles. These restrictions are an inherent part of the means testing involved in Dibao eligibility screening, but one serious consequence is that they limit Dibao recipients' ability to have social interactions and look for and maintain jobs. Fieldwork evidence suggests that many Dibao recipients conduct job search through social connections (Liu,

2011; Solinger, 2015a). However, many Dibao recipients do not have phones or computers, thus it is very difficult to stay connected with former colleagues and other social contacts. Several Dibao recipients interviewed across cities in 2007 said that, in order to save money, they did not make outgoing phone calls from their landline phones and only answered incoming calls (Han, 2012). It is easy to imagine how this might restrict their job-seeking efforts. With many job openings increasingly posted online only, the lack of a computer serves as another barrier to Dibao recipients' job search activities.

Related to asset ownership restrictions are local rules regarding recipients' behavior or lifestyle choices that serve as similar deterrents. Indeed, some of these rules restrict Dibao recipients from pursuing better life opportunities and trap them in deeper or chronic poverty. For example, through fieldwork in several cities, Solinger (2009, 2010) discovered that some local governments prohibited Dibao recipients from sending their children to better schools or from trying to run a family business. In some cities, owning a family business, regardless of its profits or losses, makes people ineligible for Dibao benefits. She argued that, through these restrictions, Dibao in effect denied recipient families and their children any opportunity for upward mobility and confined them to long-term destitution.

The third policy design barrier is that, in the current Chinese system, eligibility for other social assistance programs, such as medical, education, housing, and temporary assistance, is often tied to eligibility for Dibao, with Dibao eligibility serving as the de facto gatekeeper for anyone to be considered for other types of assistance. Needless to say, this serves as a strong disincentive for Dibao recipients to move off the welfare roll, for fear that they would not be able to get any additional help for other needs, such as healthcare and education.

Both Dibao recipients themselves and local Dibao officials acknowledged the strong work disincentive associated with the tied eligibility for various social assistance programs. Through individual and focus group interviews, Xu (2013) found that many Dibao recipients considered some supplementary benefits— such as medical, education, and housing assistance—more important than Dibao itself, and thought that losing eligibility for all of these benefits at once was too risky, especially when there were no stable jobs available.

Among the sample of 1,209 Dibao recipients in six cities in 2007, Han and Guo (2012) found that a quarter of the respondents wished that they could still be eligible for other welfare benefits such as education and health assistance even if they lost eligibility for Dibao after finding a job. Being able to continue to access and receive other benefits would be a great incentive for them to seek and maintain employment.

Fourth, some local governments have explicitly or implicitly required Dibao recipients to "stay off the streets" and have discouraged them from becoming vendors or taking up temporary jobs. Government officials are afraid that such activities may disrupt "normal" economic activities or make the streets look untidy, especially during periods of important political and social events when it is vital for the government to showcase a peaceful, orderly, and prosperous Chinese society. Such evidence is not apparent from large-scale surveys but is offered through fieldwork, in-depth interviews, and focus groups among local officials and Dibao recipients (Solinger, 2013; Xu, 2013).

In sum, these different elements of policy design join forces and serve as deterrents for Dibao recipients to move from welfare to work. Solinger (2009) referred to these difficulties faced by Dibao recipients to obtain work as "enforced worklessness" and concluded that the Dibao program indeed tripped up recipients and failed to enable them to become self-sufficient (pp. 328–329). The same concerns have been shared by some policymakers who worry that Dibao's public image may shift from being a safety net to a welfare trap. A related concern is that by deterring work efforts, Dibao may serve as a vehicle for intergenerational poverty in which the next generation of welfare recipients will also rely on welfare for their livelihood.

LOCAL INITIATIVES TO PROMOTE WORK EFFORTS

In an effort to facilitate welfare-to-work transitions, many local governments have experimented with policies and programs that aim to promote and sustain work efforts among Dibao recipients. These initiatives can be classified into four types according to their policy goals: punitive, protective, incentive, and supportive. These initiatives are presented in Table 6.2 and discussed in this section. Unfortunately, the evaluation evidence regarding their effectiveness is scarce and is thus much needed in future research endeavors. Local governments could collaborate with research scholars in designing and carrying out robust evaluation projects to assess the effectiveness of these welfare-to-work initiatives so that they can be incorporated into future policy reforms.

The first and most traditional type of welfare-to-work initiative is punitive in nature. Typically, Dibao recipients with work abilities are required to participate in "mandatory voluntary" community work or job-training programs. Sometimes they are also asked to take certain jobs recommended by local Dibao officials or employment agencies. If the Dibao recipients fail to participate in such programs or refuse to take the referred jobs for no legitimate reason several times, they can lose their Dibao eligibility. Recipients who take the referred job but later are dismissed by their employer owing to their own inadequacies or misconduct cannot reclaim their Dibao eligibility (Xu, 2013). Beijing has been carrying out this initiative since 2004, and many other cities have adopted similar measures. For example, Han and Guo (2012) found that nearly two thirds of the 1,209 Dibao recipients studied in six cities in 2007 reported that they had participated in voluntary activities organized by community or neighborhood

Table 6.2. Local Welfare-to-Work Initiatives

Type/Goal	Sample Approaches
Punitive	Losing Dibao eligibility if recipients fail to participate in "mandatory voluntary" community work or refuse to take jobs referred by Dibao officials or employment agencies
Protective	Higher income disregard, especially for families with ill, disabled, or older members; offering differentiated benefit levels according to work ability
Incentive	Gradual reduction in Dibao benefits after recipients find a job; exemption of income earned at minimum wage or another predetermined level
Supportive	Providing skills training, job referral, and support for establishing small businesses; offering special job search assistance to individuals with disabilities, through community employment service centers

offices, and those who had not participated in such activities were mainly those with disability or poor health or were older.

This punitive approach to improving welfare-to-work transition is similar in nature to the 5-year time limit imposed on welfare recipients through the 1996 welfare reform implemented in the United States. Research shows that, as a result of welfare reform, particularly its time limit component, employment and earnings of its target population have increased while welfare caseloads have decreased. However, the effects on income are mixed, as increased earnings are often offset by reduced welfare benefits (Moffitt, 2003a; Ziliak, 2016). These findings offer caution regarding the punitive approach adopted in Chinese and other international contexts.

The second type of initiative is more protective of Dibao recipients' economic resources and fosters motivation for engaging in work activities. It takes into consideration the specific health conditions and work abilities of Dibao recipients. One approach in this type of initiative is to adopt a higher income disregard, especially for families with ill, disabled, or older members, so that those with greater needs have a greater chance of being eligible for Dibao benefits. For example, in 2015, Beijing began to disregard household income equivalent to the Dibao line for families whose members had serious disease or disability when deciding Dibao eligibility and amount of benefits. An additional disregard of income equivalent to 50% of the Dibao line was applied if the family had an older member (Lan, 2015). Another approach is to offer differentiated benefit levels to those with different work abilities. For example, since 2004, Beijing has raised the benefit level by 10% for children 16 or younger, adults 70 and older, and persons with disabilities and by 15% for the "Three Without" (Sanwu, i.e., without working ability, income source, or family support) households (Xu, 2013).

The third type of initiative offers direct incentives for Dibao recipients to seek and sustain work activities. The most prominent approaches in this type include gradual reduction of Dibao benefits after recipients find a job and disregarding of minimum-wage income or income at another predetermined level. For example, in 2002, Shanghai was the first city to implement a gradual reduction of Dibao benefits for those who found a job. In 2003, the period of gradual reduction was extended from 1–3 months to 2–6 months. The exact reduction period of benefits varied according to the entitled amount of Dibao benefits as well as income earned through the new job (Shanghai Bureau of Civil Affairs, 2003). To provide incentives for Dibao recipients to pursue and keep jobs, Beijing and Shanghai both disregard a proportion of earned income so that families may still qualify for Dibao benefits even after a member finds a job. Beijing deducts the difference between the minimum wage and the Dibao line in calculating total household income (Xu, 2013). Shanghai discounts the equivalent of minimum wage when determining the entitled Dibao amount and in recent years has adjusted this amount biannually (Shanghai Bureau of Civil Affairs, 2015). Since 2007, Hunan province has allowed recipients to keep their Dibao benefits for 2 months after finding a job (Xu, 2013).

The last type of initiative provides direct support to Dibao recipients' job search efforts. These include providing skills training, job referral, support for establishing small businesses, and offering special job search assistance to individuals with disabilities. Local governments usually implement these initiatives through establishing community employment service centers, often set up jointly by local branches of the civil affairs bureau and the human resources and social security bureau. In 2010, the Ministry of Human Resources and Social Security (MHRSS) instructed all of its local branches to integrate resources and strengthen work support for individuals facing employment challenges and emphasized this as one of the foci for the 2011–2015 period (MHRSS, 2010). However, local governments have followed this policy direction at their own pace. Thus far, only cities with more employment opportunities and greater financial capacity have implemented it. The pace has been even slower in implementing employment support for Dibao recipients, partly because of the challenges involved in coordinating the personnel and policy priorities between the civil affairs and human resources and social security departments.

Beijing was one of the first cities to establish community-level employment and social security service centers, in an effort to effectively integrate social assistance and employment services (Xu, 2013). Dongguan of Guangdong province launched its employment support program in 2014, which included providing skills training, job referrals, support for setting up small businesses, and special job search assistance to individuals with disabilities. Another approach adopted by Dongguan was the pairing of Dibao recipients looking for a job with non-recipients who were willing and capable of providing employment support (Duan, 2015).

Despite the existence of a wide array of local welfare-to-work initiatives of different types, evaluation evidence on the effectiveness of these programs remains scarce. This is partly because of the incremental and scattered nature of such initiatives, which makes systematic evaluations less likely, and partly because of the lack of coordination between local governments and research scholars in designing and monitoring the performance of these programs. The small set of existing evidence suggests limited effectiveness of these initiatives.

In a survey of 500 low-income families—437 of which were Dibao recipients—in a Shanghai community in 2009–2010, only 16% reported having participated in any skills training offered by community employment centers. Over half (55%) of the participants considered the trainings helpful, but only about a quarter said they found a job after receiving the training, while the majority of those surveyed were unable to move from welfare to work (Gao, 2015). Based on a survey of Dibao recipients in three cities in 2012, Xu (2013) found a lack of available employment training services and limited effectiveness of these services in helping Dibao recipients find jobs. Among the 2,550 respondents who reported information regarding their employment, only 12% received any job or skills training, and among those, half considered the training effective. Among those who received any training, 4% reported having found a job but not taking it, 28% tried to look for a job but failed, and the other 67% did not look for a job at all.

Information collected through focus groups conducted among local officials and Dibao recipients further demonstrated the disconnection between some of the work support programs and the reality faced by Dibao families. For example, the skills and job-training programs offered often lacked specificity and were not tailored to the needs of the Dibao recipients, leading to ineffective results. The referred jobs were mostly temporary and unstable, without offering social insurance coverage, and were demanding in time commitment. These were far from what the Dibao recipients expected from a job and often took recipients away from necessary family care responsibilities (Xu, 2013).

SUMMARY AND IMPLICATIONS

This chapter offers a not-so-promising picture of welfare dependency and welfare-to-work transitions for Dibao recipients. While the majority of Dibao recipients are working-age adults, most engage in limited work activities and have remained on welfare for a relatively long time, unwillingly being labeled "welfare dependents." Even among those who do work, most hold informal, irregular, and menial jobs that do not guarantee long-term economic stability and sufficiency. Many localities require Dibao recipients to participate in "mandatory voluntary work" as a way to ensure some social contribution from them in exchange for welfare receipt as well as to prevent underground employment. However, these jobs tend to be time-consuming, unproductive, and degrading to Dibao recipients. They also take valuable time away from family care responsibilities and other potentially more meaningful work pursuits.

Existing empirical research has revealed many barriers for Dibao recipients to moving from welfare to work. These include limited employability at the individual level due to poor health, low levels of education, lack of skills, middle age, long history of unemployment, and lack of financial or social capital. At the household level, Dibao recipients often have heavy family care responsibilities, especially those with sick or disabled family members as well as children and elders. At the community level, the lack of childcare and senior care services and the stigma from neighbors and local officials further hinder Dibao recipients' employment efforts. At the policy level, the treatment of any additional income at the 100% marginal tax rate, restrictions on asset ownership and lifestyle choices, tied eligibility for Dibao and other social assistance programs, and pressure from some localities on Dibao recipients to "stay off the streets" all join forces to limit recipients' motivation and the opportunities for moving from welfare to work. Such employment challenges for welfare recipients are especially acute given the newly estimated broader trends in rising unemployment and decreasing labor force participation that paint a darker picture than that reported in official statistics (Feng, Hu, & Moffitt, 2015).

In recent years, local governments have initiated an array of welfare-to-work programs in an effort to promote employment among Dibao recipients. These range from punitive approaches (such as removing Dibao eligibility if recipients fail to participate in "mandatory voluntary work") to protective measures (such as gradual reduction of benefits after recipients find a job) to those offering direct incentives for seeking and keeping jobs (such as the adoption of higher income disregard), and to direct services that support employment (such as offering skills training and job referrals). Most of these are promising initiatives, yet the small body of existing evidence suggests that the job-training programs have limited effectiveness in helping Dibao recipients obtain or maintain employment. This set of evidence highlights the long-term challenges faced by many similar social assistance programs around the world that hope to reduce welfare dependency and succeed in welfare-to-work policies and programs.

Taken together, these findings offer important policy implications for how to better address the continued challenges in promoting welfare-to-work transitions. First and foremost, it is crucial to understand the unique life situations and constraints faced by many Dibao recipients. The individual-, household-, and community-level barriers faced by many of these individuals need to be addressed before welfare-to-work initiatives can have any concrete, meaningful impact. For example, many Dibao recipients have poor health or chronic illness, or they need to take care of children, elders, or sick family members. Without sufficient healthcare and education support, including adequate health insurance for the poor, free and good-quality early education and public education, and community services and facilities for childcare and senior care, it is impossible for these Dibao recipients to take up jobs that would take them away from these family or self-care responsibilities. One way to understand the exact life challenges and constraints faced by Dibao families is to ask them directly and address those particular needs. This very simple approach has been proven to be cost-effective and to have long-lasting effects by recent evaluation evidence from the United States (Kirp, 2015).

Second, it is also important to conduct a careful examination of Dibao's policy design and address any components that offer inherent disincentives for recipients to move off the welfare roll. For example, the strict means testing which essentially treats any additional income—especially earned income—at a 100% marginal tax rate is understandably discouraging for Dibao recipients' work efforts. While this is not unique to China, the unstable and irregular job prospects faced by Dibao recipients could be even more threatening if recipients are afraid of losing their Dibao eligibility permanently or for a long time after landing a short-term job. Similarly, restrictions on certain assets (such as phones and computers) and life choices (such as sending children to a higher-quality, more expensive school) are not only demeaning but in effect deprive these families of job opportunities and possible upward mobility, especially for their children. Some local policies, such as the requirement that Dibao recipients "stay off the streets," counter initiatives that promote work activities in this group. These policies need to be reflected on and considered in a more holistic framework in Dibao's future reforms.

One example of a more flexible design of a social assistance program is Brazil's Bolsa Família Program, a large conditional cash transfer (CCT) program that provides cash assistance to poor families and promotes human development, especially in education and health. This program uses unverified means testing at the municipal level to determine eligibility. Though mostly relying on self-reported income information, the application form also asks about family consumption patterns, which are used to cross-check the reported income information and to gauge families' consumption needs. Brazil also has a federal database that contains information on formal-sector workers' employment status and earnings, which is also used for cross-checking self-reported income. While the Brazilian system is not perfect and still means-testing in nature, it offers more trust and dignity to welfare recipients and fewer direct disincentives against employment pursuits.

One unique feature of the Chinese social assistance system is the tied eligibility of Dibao and its supplementary programs, which is convenient for implementation of such programs but offers strong disincentive for recipients to leave Dibao. In reality, many Dibao recipients are more afraid of losing these supplementary benefits than they are of losing Dibao itself. Future reforms should consider untying these eligibility rules and offering different eligibility standards for families with unique needs such as healthcare, education, and housing. For example, in the United States, the primary health insurance program for the poor, Medicaid, has a much higher income disregard level than the primary welfare program, Temporary Assistance to Needy Families (TANF). The necessary costs for meeting these important needs other than maintaining minimum livelihood should be considered.

A third policy implication is that, for any welfare-to-work initiatives to have a real impact, it is important for the MCA and MHRSS and their local branches to carry out more concerted collaborations (Xu, 2013). Thus far, these efforts have been fragmented, with the MCA in charge of social assistance provision and the MHRSS in charge of employment promotion. Some of the contradictions observed in the policy design—such as the "stay off the streets" requirement versus welfare-to-work initiatives—may well be the result of this fragmentation. Interviews with government officials in both departments at the central and local levels confirm this tension and inefficiency, yet there appears to be no clear indication that a more coordinated approach has been planned (Solinger, 2015a). Without addressing this bureaucratic fragmentation, the promotion of welfare-to-work transitions among Dibao recipients could be costly yet futile.

Finally, there needs to be more systematic evaluation of the effectiveness of the various welfare-to-work initiatives so that future reforms can incorporate effective measures into policy changes. In particular, the initiatives that offer protection, incentives, and support could be evaluated and enhanced to help promote successful transitions from welfare to work. Close collaboration between local governments and the research community in the evaluation design and process would help provide timely and valuable scientific evidence.

Meanwhile, China can learn from other countries that have had success in implementing work support programs. For example, many countries have implemented "make work pay" programs such as the Earned Income Tax Credit (EITC) in the United States and South Korea and the Working Tax Credit in the United Kingdom that are effective in both alleviating poverty and promoting work efforts. These programs operate as a refundable tax credit to subsidize workers in low- and middle-income families, providing both additional income and work incentive. The EITC has been expanded drastically several times and is currently the most effective anti-poverty program in the United States. South Korea adopted the EITC policy in 2008 (Gao, Yoo, Yang, & Zhai, 2011; Gao & Zhai, 2012; Kim, Zou, Joo, & Sherraden, 2011). Given its effectiveness and relative low cost of implementation, China should also consider adopting a similar measure as one of the main anti-poverty programs that could have long-term positive effects.

Another effective approach has been for the government to work collaboratively with community and other non-governmental organizations (NGOs) to improve the effectiveness and efficiency in delivering welfare-to-work services. Typically, the government provides the majority or part of the funding for these initiatives, but the NGOs have lots of autonomy in program design and service delivery. Such autonomy could foster creativity and better outcomes. These NGOs are usually subject to rigorous transparency and accountability demands and thus may be more efficient. Local communities in collaboration with NGOs have the potential to build a solidarity economy that enhances both economic security and labor force participation for low-income individuals and families (Dacheux & Goujon, 2012).

In sum, welfare-to-work initiatives have plenty of political and public support that is deeply rooted in the high value placed on work in Chinese culture. Future Dibao reforms should build on this wide support to design policies and programs that can bring real change to the economic conditions and life opportunities of poor families and their children.

7

FAMILY EXPENDITURES AND
HUMAN CAPITAL INVESTMENT

Like all people around the world who are struggling with poverty, Dibao families have meager resources and are constantly making hard choices about consumption. Internationally, a growing number of poverty scholars have argued that examining consumption yields a more accurate estimate of living standards than is achieved by focusing on income (e.g., Blank, 2006; Davis, 2005; Kaushal, Gao, & Waldfogel, 2007; Meyer & Sullivan, 2008; Wang, Cheng, & Smyth, 2015; Wong & Yu, 2002). Consumption choices are especially hard for poor families given their tight budgets. It can be difficult to decide whether to meet short-term survival needs by paying for food or rent, or to invest in human capital by paying for education and health. The extra money these families receive from welfare may enable them to make such choices with some ease.

How do Dibao families prioritize their consumption needs and spend their Dibao money? Do they use it to meet basic survival needs, invest in human capital, or improve their quality of life? Do they spend it on so-called temptation goods, such as tobacco and alcohol, or pay for necessary gifts for family and friends? Do urban and rural Dibao recipients make different or similar consumption choices? In this chapter, I first describe the consumption patterns of Dibao families and then summarize empirical evidence based on large-scale household survey data to help understand the possible effects of receiving Dibao on family expenditures.

FIVE TYPES OF FAMILY EXPENDITURES

The analysis and discussion in this chapter will examine the following five types of family expenditures. First, expenditures that mainly help families meet survival needs include those for food, clothing, housing and utilities, transportation, and communication. Housing expenditures further include rent, renovations, and maintenance fees. Examining these expenditures is of vital importance, as helping poor families to maintain subsistence is the central goal of Dibao and many other similar means-tested cash transfer programs. Do Dibao families use the money to support their basic livelihood? Focusing on this type of family expenditure will help address this fundamental question.

Second, expenditures on health and education focus on human capital investment, especially for children. Specifically, health expenses include medicine, medical care, health supplies, nutrient supplements, and other health-related expenses. Education expenses include textbooks and tuition and fees for compulsory and noncompulsory education, day care center fees, continuing education, private tutoring, training classes, school lodging, and other education-related expenses. This chapter will pay special attention to expenditures related to human capital investment, as they serve as an effective tool for reducing intergenerational transmission of poverty. As mentioned in earlier chapters, many conditional cash transfer (CCT) programs around the world make cash transfers conditional on investment in human capital or actions related to human development. It is important to understand whether unconditional cash transfer (UCT) programs such as Dibao can help achieve the same goals without explicitly requiring human capital investment as a condition for receiving benefits.

Third, expenditures on improving quality of life include spending on facilities, services, and leisure. Specifically, expenditures for facilities and services include those for durable and non-durable goods as well as fees paid for home services, such as cleaning and cooking. Leisure spending includes purchase of leisure products, such as a television or computer, and spending on leisure activities, such as sightseeing or going to a movie. As the Chinese society becomes richer and more modernized, people tend to spend more on such quality-of-life items or activities. Does receiving Dibao enable poor families to follow this trend and spend more on improving their quality of life? Or is the Dibao amount so meager that these families cannot afford to spend it on such luxuries?

Fourth, expenditures on so-called temptation goods, such as alcohol and tobacco, often garner special attention in the international welfare literature (Dasso & Fernandez, 2014; Evans & Popova, 2014). Policymakers and the public often worry that poor families use cash transfer money to purchase temptation goods instead of providing necessities or investing in their children. Do Dibao recipients use their Dibao money on alcohol and tobacco consumption?

Lastly, transfer expenditures include spending on gifts to family, friends, and relatives and necessary social insurance contributions. On the one hand, welfare benefits may enable poor families to afford such expenses, which are important for maintaining social networks and ensuring long-term social protection through pensions and health insurance. On the other hand, the meager welfare amount may not be enough for these families to afford such transfer expenses. In addition, families on welfare may be reluctant to spend money on these items for fear of public scrutiny. They may also be isolated from social connections due to the stigma and shame associated with receiving Dibao benefits, especially in clear view of their former colleagues (Solinger, 2011).

These five types of family expenditures serve different purposes and meet different consumption needs. While there is no complete evidence on how receiving Dibao might affect patterns of each type of family expenditure, in this chapter, I gather the existing evidence on the possible effects of Dibao receipt on family expenditures and report the findings whenever they are available.

CONSUMPTION PATTERNS OF DIBAO FAMILIES

Before trying to examine the possible link between Dibao participation and family expenditures, it is helpful to understand the basic consumption patterns of Dibao families. This set of descriptive evidence reveals different consumption patterns between urban and rural Dibao families. In urban areas, expenditures on food and other survival necessities remain the largest consumption item for Dibao families, while many also spend substantial portions of their resources on education and healthcare. In rural areas, healthcare is the major expenditure for most Dibao families, partly because most rural families can get food from farm production and thus do not need to pay for it, and partly because many rural families still lack health insurance and have to pay for healthcare out of pocket. For both urban and rural Dibao families, expenses for education and healthcare are particularly high for families with children and whose members have severe or chronic disease.

Focusing on urban areas, Hu, Gao, and Cui (2013) tracked 33 Dibao families in Jinan of Shandong province for over a year (November 2008 to December 2009) and studied their detailed expenditure patterns. They found that, while food expenditures accounted for 35 to 38% of these families' monthly spending, half of the families had education expenses, which accounted for approximately 30 to 75% of their annual family expenditure. Five of the 33 families had health expenditures that accounted for about 22 to 51% of their annual family expenditures. None of these families were found to have any leisure expenses, such as sightseeing or going to a movie.

Based on a sample of 358 low-income families with school-age children from Kaifeng city in Henan province in 2008, Wang (2009) found that, on average, Dibao families devoted 38% of total expenditures to food, 28% to healthcare, 21% to education, and 11% to housing and utilities. Most of the education expenses were for tuition and fees for high school, vocational school, or higher education as well as for textbooks and other learning materials for junior middle school, which is part of compulsory education in China.

Using 2012 survey data from 1,200 Dibao families in three cities in Shandong province, Gao, Chen, and Cui (2013) found that food was the largest expenditure item (25.7% of total family expenditures), which was followed closely by healthcare expenses (25.6%). Contributions to pensions and health insurance were the next big expenditure, accounting for 17% of total family expenditures, followed by education expenses for children (12%) and housing and utility expenses (9%). Based on fieldwork in Beijing and Lanzhou, one wealthy and one poor city, Mok and Wong (2011) demonstrated disproportionately high educational cost borne by families in poorer regions and additional education-related hardships endured by these families.

Indeed, many urban Dibao recipients consider healthcare and education their main expenditure burden. In a 2012 survey of 2,550 working-age Dibao recipients in three cities, Xu (2013) found that 16% of respondents attributed their decline into poverty to medical expenses, and 9% said that they became poor because of their children's education expenses. Over half of these respondents said that Dibao could only help them cover up to one third of total family expenditures, with another 30% of respondents saying that Dibao helped cover about half of their total expenses.

Qualitative interview data offer vivid details about the multiple challenges faced by many Dibao families. In 2007–2008, commissioned by the Ministry of Civil Affairs (MCA), a team of researchers from Remin University of China carried out in-depth interviews with 28 Dibao families and 8 local Dibao officials across six cities. They also conducted focus groups among local Dibao officials in four of these cities. These interview and focus group records were edited into a book (Han, 2012). While protecting the identity and privacy of interviewees, the book retained all other original information collected during the fieldwork and offers rich first-hand qualitative data to the research community and the public.

The Dibao recipients interviewed in this study were asked to describe their monthly income and consumption patterns. Many identified healthcare and education as the major expenses, on top of scrambling to pay for basic survival necessities such as food, rent, and utilities. As documented in another study (Lora-Wainwright, 2011), many Dibao recipients avoided seeing a doctor or visiting the hospital unless it was absolutely necessary. For example, one 34-year old Dibao recipient in Beijing said that all four members of his family were struggling with health problems: his wife had cerebral vasospasm, a chronic condition; he had gastroenteritis; and their 2-year old twins often had health problems. He lost a job assigned to him in the community police station after he developed a sudden illness. He and his wife both stayed home to take care of the twins. In the previous year, he reported,

My two kids got sick and spent over 2,000 yuan. [Medical assistance] only covered about 400 yuan. . . . In the end we paid about 1,500 yuan out of pocket . . . 1,500 yuan! That's over two months' Dibao money. Two months' meals. Healthcare is really scary. (Han, 2012, p. 15; interviewee, 34-year-old Mr. Kong)

Often Dibao families had to choose between paying for healthcare and education given their meager resources and tight budget. Mr. Ren, another interviewee in the same study, chose to prioritize education for his 18-year old son, who attended a vocational high school. Mr. Ren had chronic stomach disease and arthritis but rarely saw a doctor. He was much more concerned about how to pay the tuition and fees for his son, as the fall semester was imminent. Their family of three received a total of 600 yuan monthly from Dibao. He said,

You see, it's almost September 1st, but, honestly, I barely have money for food. . . . I do not know where my next meal is from. I get help from this person and that person. . . . When the semester starts, I have to pay over 3,000 yuan—2,200 yuan for tuition, and the rest are fees for textbooks and others. . . . How can I pull together that much money? (Han, 2012, p. 111; interviewee, 44-year-old Mr. Ren)

Many Dibao families not only face high financial burdens paying for healthcare and education but also do their best to minimize other living costs. For example, Mr. Ren also said,

No, we don't have any Internet expenses, not at all. Phone bill, yes. Basic monthly charge is 21.6 yuan. Then, others can call me, I will answer, but I won't make outgoing phone calls. So just 21.6 yuan per month. (Han, 2012, p. 108; interviewee, 44-year-old Mr. Ren)

In rural China, the largest expenditure for Dibao families is often healthcare. Chang, Chang, and Yuan (2012) used 2008 survey data from 200 Dibao families in the rural areas of Shanghai and found that the primary expense for these families was healthcare (averaging 40% of total family expenditures), followed by food (28%) and education (12%). Dibao families also had necessary expenditures for gifts to family, friends, and relatives (7% of total family expenditures), utilities (5%), and transportation and communication (3%).

My calculations from household survey data collected from 9,107 rural families from five provinces (Jiangxi, Anhui, Henan, Shanxi, and Gansu) of central and western China in 2010 show that healthcare expenses accounted for 37% of Dibao families' total expenditures, followed by food (22%), housing and utilities (17%), and education (10%). Another 5% was spent on elder support and gifts to family, friends, and relatives. Healthcare and education expenses were especially high for families with these needs. Specifically, among families with at least one member who had a chronic disease, healthcare expenses accounted for 44% of total family expenditures. Among families with school-age children, education expenses accounted for 23% of total family expenditures. These figures highlight the insufficiency of Dibao benefits to fully support these families and the urgency to offer appropriate health and education assistance to them.

DIBAO RECEIPT AND FAMILY EXPENDITURES

Keeping the consumption patterns of Dibao families in mind, I now turn to examine the possible effects of Dibao receipt on family expenditures. Faced with a tight budget and multiple competing needs, how do Dibao families use their welfare money? What do they prioritize when making hard choices between meeting survival needs and investing in education and health? Do they spend their Dibao money on improving their quality of life, on temptation goods such as alcohol and tobacco, or on gifts to others?

Empirically, selection bias remains the primary challenge for teasing out the causal link between welfare participation and family expenditure outcomes in the global welfare literature. In the Chinese context, families who receive Dibao may be systematically different from their non-recipient peers, and any difference in their family expenditure outcomes might be due to such systematic differences instead of receiving Dibao per se. Internationally, a growing body of development economics literature used matching methods to address the issue of selection bias and estimate the possible effects of welfare programs and other policies and interventions (Dehejia & Wahba, 2002; Jalan & Ravallion, 2003; Rosenbaum & Rubin, 1983).

To understand the possible effects of Dibao receipt on family expenditure patterns, a set of recent studies have used large-scale household survey data and a propensity score matching (PSM) method to identify comparable non-recipients who have similar observed characteristics to those of welfare recipients. The effects of welfare participation are estimated by comparing the outcomes of the welfare recipients with those of their matched non-recipient peers. It is important to note that, like any other matching methods, PSM can only take into consideration observable characteristics of these families that are available in the data sets, which are never exhaustive and cannot account for all the possible factors associated with their welfare participation. These estimates, therefore, are not strictly causal and need to be interpreted with caution. However, they provide a more accurate evaluation of the effects of Dibao receipt than estimates from models without matching. In addition, a series of recent studies in both medical and welfare research showed that PSM consistently yields results that are very close to those based on experimental designs, manifesting its rigor in approximating causal effects (Diaz & Handa, 2006; Handa & Maluccio, 2008; Kitsios et al., 2015; Zahoor et al., 2015).

This set of studies showed that urban Dibao families prioritized spending on health and education, two main expenses of human capital investment, over other types of expenditures, while rural Dibao families prioritized healthcare but not education. Meeting survival needs was not a priority use of Dibao money for either urban or rural recipients, which suggests that these families may be maintaining subsistence while having to meet urgent health or education needs. In both urban and rural China, Dibao receipt was associated with reduced spending on leisure. While urban Dibao was not found to be linked to expenditures on temptation goods or gifts to others, rural Dibao receipt was associated with reduced spending on alcohol, tobacco, gifts to others, and social insurance contributions.

URBAN DIBAO: FOCUSING ON HUMAN CAPITAL INVESTMENT

Focusing on urban Dibao, my colleagues and I (Gao, Zhai & Garfinkel, 2010; Gao et al., 2014) used the China Household Income Project (CHIP) 2002 and 2007 urban data and a PSM method to examine the association between Dibao receipt and family expenditure patterns. Results from the 2 years under study were remarkably consistent. Dibao helped lift recipient families' overall expenditure level and, in particular, their spending on health and education. Specifically, as compared to their peers who were non-recipients but similar in other demographic and socioeconomic characteristics, Dibao helped enable recipient families to afford medicine, medical care, tuition and fees for noncompulsory education, private tutoring for children, and textbooks.

Figures 7.1–7.3 summarize the magnitude of these estimated effects as measured by percentage changes in the expenditure item associated with Dibao receipt. Only statistically significant results are presented. As shown in Figure 7.1, in both 2002 and 2007, Dibao receipt was associated with increased total family expenditures as well as expenditures on health, education, and miscellaneous items. The effect magnitudes were consistently larger in 2007 than in 2002 (except for miscellaneous items), a finding suggesting that the expanded Dibao in 2007 played a more powerful role in supporting family expenditures than in 2002.

Specifically, in 2007, urban Dibao receipt helped raise total family expenditure level by 10.3%, a 3-percentage point increase from 2002. The effects of Dibao on health and education expenditures were even more striking. In 2007, Dibao receipt was associated with a 42.7% increase in health expenditures, an almost 10-percentage point increase from 2002. Dibao also increased education expenditures of recipient families by 31.3% in 2007, which was a 5-percentage point increase from 2002. These results suggest that urban Dibao recipients prioritized

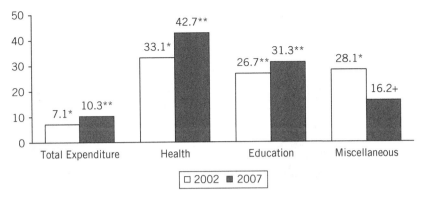

Figure 7.1. Effects of urban Dibao receipt on total family expenditures and major categories, 2002 and 2007 (measured as percent [%] of average expenditure levels). $**p < 0.01$, $*p < 0.05$, $+ p < 0.10$. Sources: Results for 2002 are from Gao, Zhai, and Garfinkel (2010). Results for 2007 are from Gao, Zhai, Yang, and Li (2014). Both studies used China Household Income Project (CHIP) urban survey data.

human capital investment to a great extent as compared to their non-recipient peers.

Figure 7.2 presents the association between Dibao receipt and detailed health expenditure patterns based on CHIP 2002 and 2007 urban estimates. The positive effects of receiving Dibao on health expenditures were mainly present for two items—medicine and medical care. Specifically, urban Dibao enabled recipient families to spend 32.1% more on medicine in 2002 and 48.9% more in 2007 as compared to their non-recipient peers. In 2007, urban Dibao recipients also spent 38.2% more on medical care than did non-recipients; however, this effect was not detected in 2002. The larger positive effect of Dibao receipt on medicine and medical care in 2007 as compared to 2002 may be due to the expanded Dibao benefits during this period, but it could also be due to rising healthcare costs, which forced families to spend more on these items. In contrast, in neither year was Dibao receipt found to be associated with increased spending on nutrient supplements, health supplies, or other non-specified health expenses. This suggests that urban Dibao families mostly spent whatever was necessary to treat their health problems but not beyond this.

Figure 7.3 shows the magnitude of estimated association between urban Dibao receipt and detailed education expenditures. Urban Dibao helped boost recipient families' spending on noncompulsory education tuition and fees in both 2002 (by 38%) and 2007 (by 25.6%), a significant help to these families given the high cost associated with noncompulsory education in China. In 2007, urban Dibao also enabled recipient families to pay for more textbooks (by 27.8%) and private tutoring (by 45.6%). These effects were not found for 2002.

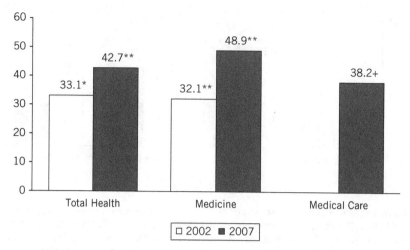

Figure 7.2. Effects of urban Dibao receipt on health expenditures, 2002 and 2007 (measured as percent [%] of average expenditure levels). $**p < 0.01$, $*p < 0.05$, $+ p < 0.10$. Sources: Results for 2002 are from Gao, Zhai, and Garfinkel (2010). Results for 2007 are from Gao, Zhai, Yang, and Li (2014). Both studies used China Household Income Project (CHIP) urban survey data.

These results are robust based on multiple sensitivity tests. Further, among the urban Dibao recipients, those receiving a high benefit amount (i.e., above the median benefit amount) were able to raise their total family expenditure level as well as spending on health and education as compared to their non-recipient

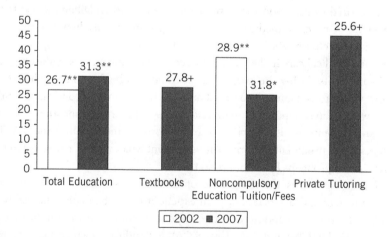

Figure 7.3. Effects of urban Dibao receipt on education expenditures, 2002 and 2007 (measured as percent [%] of average expenditure levels). $**p < 0.01$, $*p < 0.05$, $+ p < 0.10$. Sources: Results for 2002 are from Gao, Zhai, and Garfinkel (2010). Results for 2007 are from Gao, Zhai, Yang, and Li (2014). Both studies used China Household Income Project (CHIP) urban survey data.

peers, while those receiving a low amount (i.e., below the median benefit amount) were only able to improve their spending on health, but not education.

These findings may be partly due to the additional income obtained from Dibao benefits, which enabled these families to spend more on health and education, but they also have particular pertinence to the Chinese cultural and social context. On the one hand, it is well known that Chinese culture values education greatly and parents are expected or often feel obligated to do their best to invest in their children's education, regardless of family income level or social class. Research on Chinese and other Asian-American immigrants has found that low-income parents are just as willing as their middle- and high- income peers to invest a significant proportion of their resources in children's education (Lee & Zhou, 2004, 2015). On the other hand, the strict screening and public display of the applicants list by local government officials implementing the Dibao program places extra pressure on recipients to spend their money in a socially acceptable manner, which in the Chinese context translates to spending on education and healthcare.

Consistent with this cultural and social context, our results also showed that, in 2007, urban Dibao receipt was associated with reduced spending on leisure activities (by 30%), such as sightseeing or going to a movie. Meanwhile, it is interesting to note that we did not find significant increases in food expenditures associated with urban Dibao receipt, an increase one would naturally expect for welfare recipients and is indeed one of the intended goals of the Dibao program. The bulk of evidence from CCT programs in Latin America, by contrast, suggests a more than proportionate growth in food consumption as a result of receiving the cash transfers (Attanasio & Mesnard, 2006; Barrientos, 2013; Fiszbein et al., 2009; Hoddinott & Skoufias, 2004). This trend was not identified in most studies of UCT programs like Dibao, except those specifically targeting food assistance, like the Supplemental Nutrition Assistance Program (SNAP) in the United States (Aizer et al., 2014; Gao, Kaushal, & Waldfogel, 2009; Kaushal & Gao, 2011). Our results, however, strongly echo the finding that many CCT programs help boost total household consumption (Rawlings & Rubin, 2005).

RURAL DIBAO: PRIORITIZING HEALTHCARE OVER EDUCATION

Existing literature on the possible effects of rural Dibao receipt on family expenditures is scarce, mainly because of the lack of available large-scale household survey data. In a recent study, my colleagues and I (Han, Gao, & Xu, 2016) used survey data from 9,107 households from five provinces of central and western China in 2010 to investigate the possible effects of receiving Dibao on rural families. We found that Dibao helped enable poor families to obtain healthcare in rural China, but failed to lift education spending among these families, a finding that is different from the urban case. In fact, only health expenditures were boosted significantly by rural Dibao receipt (by 25%) among all main expenditure categories, and education expenditures were not significantly affected. In addition, rural Dibao receipt was associated with decreased family expenditures on clothing, transportation and communication, tobacco and alcohol, gifts to friends and relatives, social insurance contribution, and miscellaneous items.

These findings suggest that, once they receive Dibao, poor rural families tend to prioritize healthcare over education and other consumption demands, reflecting the serious unmet health needs among poor families in rural China despite the launching of the New Rural Cooperative Medical Scheme (NRCMS) in 2002 and its expansions since then. In fact, out-of-pocket costs for healthcare in rural China have kept rising. In 2008, 31% of rural patients among the poorest quintile should have received inpatient treatment but could not be admitted to hospitals because of lack of financial resources (Ministry of Health, 2009). Meanwhile, despite its broad population coverage, the NRCMS has been unable to reduce the financial burden of healthcare for rural families substantially because of its low reimbursement rate, failure of referral system, inefficient fee-for-service payment schemes, unreasonable incentive to providers, and supplier-induced demand for unnecessary care (Lei & Lin, 2009; Liang, Guo, Jin, Peng, & Zhang, 2012; Liu & Tsegao, 2011; Liu, Wu, & Liu, 2014; Long, Xu, Bekedam, & Tang, 2013; Long, Zhang, Xu, Tang, & Hemminki, 2010; Sun, Liu, Meng, Tang, Yu, & Tolhurst, 2009; Sun, Jackson, Carmichael, & Sleigh, 2009; Wagstaff, Lindelow, Gao, Xu, & Qian, 2009; Wang, Liu, Lu, Luo, & Liu, 2014; Yip & Hsiao, 2009).

The rural medical assistance program was designed to provide supplemental assistance to help the poor pay NRCMS premiums and cover part of medical expenses not reimbursed by the NRCMS. However, its impact on helping these families meet their healthcare needs and improve health conditions has been very limited, mainly because of its narrow population coverage, minimal benefit level, and complicated reimbursement procedures (Ren, Zeng, & Yang, 2015; Shi et al., 2010). Therefore, rural Dibao benefits may function as an additional financial source for poor families to afford necessary healthcare, as manifested by the increased health expenditures enabled by Dibao receipt.

Why was rural Dibao ineffective in helping boost recipient families' education expenditures, a result that is different from the urban Dibao? There are several possible explanations for this finding. First and foremost, existing literature has documented the drastically lower returns on education in rural than in urban settings, suggesting that rural Dibao families might be making a rational choice when they decide not to use their Dibao money to pay for education (de Brauw & Rozelle, 2007; Golley & Kong, 2013; Yao & Zhang, 2004; Zhang, 2012). Seeing no bright future for their children and lacking successful role models could seriously discourage rural Dibao families from investing in education in the first place.

Second, the financial constraint faced by poor rural families in education investment is much greater than that faced by their urban peers (Hannum, Wang, & Adams, 2008). In 2013, the per capita disposable income for rural residents was only one third of that for urban residents (National Bureau of Statistics [NBS], 2014b), while the average Dibao line for rural residents was about half that for urban residents (Ministry of Civil Affairs [MCA], 2015a), leaving rural poor families much more disadvantaged than their urban peers. Expenses on noncompulsory education (e.g., high school, vocational education, college and university) remain a particularly high financial burden for many families, but especially for poor rural families. Indeed, poor rural families often need to pay a higher proportion of their income for education of the same level—yet of lower quality—than their urban peers. The average share of education expenses in total family expenditure in urban Dibao families was 8% in 2007 based on the CHIP 2007 urban survey, while that share for rural Dibao families was 10% in 2010 based on the five-province survey in central and western China (Gao et al., 2014; Han et al., 2016). The much lower average income in rural areas makes investing in education for poor families extra challenging as compared to their urban peers.

Third, the lower returns on investment in schooling and higher education are coupled with the greater difficulty in obtaining and processing information in rural areas than in urban areas. The international literature has documented that the lack of accurate and accessible information in rural areas has led to parents' unrealistic perceived returns on education, inaccurate perceptions about their children's academic abilities, and low aspirations for the future. These negative factors often lead to underinvestment in children's education in rural areas, especially among poor families (Attanasio & Kaufmann, 2014; Bernard et al., 2014; Chiapa et al., 2012; Das, Do, & Özler, 2005; de Janvry & Sadoulet, 2006; Dizon-Ross, 2014; Hannum & Adams, 2008; Jensen, 2010; Mani et al., 2013; Mullainathan & Shafir, 2013; Nguyen, 2013).

As mentioned in Chapter 1, the education assistance program was also launched to provide supplementary education support to Dibao families in need. However, based on survey results from the five central and western provinces in 2010, only 2.6% of all students in families getting Dibao received education assistance. Among the education assistance recipients, the amount of benefits they received accounted for only 23% of their total education expenditures on average, leaving nearly all families having to borrow money to support their children's education. Dibao along with education assistance was far from adequate in enabling these poor families to pay for necessary education expenses.

Our results further show that rural Dibao receipt was associated with reduced spending on leisure and gifts to friends and relatives. These findings echo the negative effects of urban Dibao on social participation and quality of life (Gao et al., 2014; Gao, Wu, & Zhai, 2015). As discussed in Chapter 3, in applying for and receiving Dibao benefits, poor families are usually under intense scrutiny by local government officials as well as community members. The intention of this policy design is to ensure Dibao's targeting performance, but it may also create a disincentive for poor residents to enjoy life publicly or participate in social activities. Rural communities are usually more close-knit and less private than urban ones, making such adverse effects of Dibao more prominent in rural than in urban areas.

Rural Dibao recipients were also found to reduce expenses on alcohol and tobacco, two common temptation goods that are often perceived to be associated with poverty and despair (Dasso & Fernandez, 2014; Evans & Popova, 2014). These results are consistent with the international evidence from various countries in Africa, Asia, and Latin America that shows no significant effect of cash transfers on consumption of temptation goods or a significant negative effect (Evans & Popova, 2014). Such findings support the notion that concerns about using cash transfer money on alcohol and tobacco are unfounded, and poor people deserve more trust and credit for making the best decisions possible for the well-being of their families.

Another important finding for rural Dibao is that it was associated with reduced contributions to social insurance, a detrimental effect on the long-term social protection of these families. This is most likely due to the disproportionately high contribution rates for pensions and health insurance, measured as a percentage of family income, for these extremely poor families. The possible effect of Dibao receipt on urban families' contribution to social insurance was not examined in the existing quantitative literature. However, it is very likely that the same result would hold for urban Dibao. Indeed, one Dibao recipient in Beijing explained this dilemma vividly in a 2008 in-depth interview:

> People on Dibao certainly cannot afford to pay for social insurance. Otherwise they would not be able to eat. But, if you do not pay for [social insurance] contributions now, then you would get very little money in the future and it becomes another problem. (Han, 2012, p. 52; interviewee: 46-year-old Mr. Wang)

Some Dibao recipients recognize the importance of paying social insurance contributions for their healthcare and pensions, but their tight budget makes it impossible and unimaginable. A Dibao recipient in Changsha in this same study said,

> Even if I have no money, I will pay for health insurance every year, about 1,000 yuan [as my health is so bad]. Old-age insurance, I will not

pay, because I have no money at all! It costs 4,000 yuan per year, with an increase of 2% each year. . . . Where do I have that much money? (Han, 2012, p. 151; interviewee: 45-year-old Mr. Wen)

SUMMARY AND IMPLICATIONS

It is clear that both urban and rural Dibao families face high expenditure demands for healthcare and education, two major human capital investment items. These expenses are especially high for families with children and those with members who have severe or chronic disease. While Dibao has enabled urban recipient families to spend more on both of these items, it has helped rural families to pay for healthcare but not education. Meeting survival needs is not found to be a priority use of Dibao money for either urban or rural recipients, which suggests that these families may be maintaining subsistence while having to meet urgent health or education needs. In both urban and rural China, Dibao receipt was associated with reduced spending on leisure, probably because recipients were ashamed and fearful of being judged and of losing their Dibao eligibility. Rural Dibao receipt was also associated with reduced spending on alcohol, tobacco, gifts to others, and social insurance contributions, while the same effect was either not found or not examined for urban Dibao.

These findings provide important implications for future directions of Dibao. First and foremost, it is vitally important to strengthen and expand health and education support to families in need in both urban and rural China, as these families tend to struggle the most, even when receiving Dibao benefits. Careful evaluations should be conducted to understand the deficits of the current health insurance and assistance programs as well as the education support system so that their functions can be maximized. In particular, the benefit level of health insurance for the poor should be increased, and more financial support should be provided to enable them to afford health insurance and pay for out-of-pocket expenses. Compulsory education should be really compulsory—of good quality and without any fees—and noncompulsory education should be the focus of any scholarships and education assistance. The current medical and education assistance programs are marginal in scope and limited in benefit level and only provide support to a very small proportion of those in need. Such programs should be expanded in both coverage and benefit level to ensure that these families can afford basic healthcare and education.

It is especially important to emphasize the role of education as an effective anti-poverty tool, particularly against intergenerational transmission of poverty and in rural areas (Grosh et al., 2008). Education for children, especially girls, plays an important role in helping poor families escape the intergenerational poverty trap. It is distressing to learn that Dibao failed to help boost education expenditures for rural recipients because of the lower return on education investment, in addition to many other disadvantages they face compared to their urban peers. To support rural education in China, both infrastructure and teacher quality and quantity need to be improved substantially. As compulsory education is largely funded locally, which limits the quality and quantity of education in many poor areas, it is important for the central government to invest in rural education, especially in less developed regions. Public education and information should also be offered to rural residents about the importance of education for their children, while sufficient financial support should be offered to ensure educational opportunity for every rural child.

In addition, it is insufficient to only strengthen and expand health and education support, which in practice requires a large amount of extra financial resources and can take a long time to become policy. The Dibao benefit level itself should be revised and improved to reflect people's basic needs for healthcare and education. As demonstrated by the interviews cited in this chapter, each Dibao family faces its unique needs in healthcare—be it physical disability, a chronic disease, or mental illness—as well as education, childcare, elder care, or other specific demands. Applying the same Dibao assistance standard and application procedure to these very diverse families does not address the different needs of each recipient, leaving many struggling on their own. The Dibao benefit levels should be revised to reflect the different human needs and consumption demands of the various families, with the goal of ensuring that all families not only meet basic survival needs but are able to have healthcare, education, and necessary social and leisure activities.

Recent national regulations and local experimentations show promising signs of moving in this direction. At the national level, as mentioned in Chapter 2, the "Opinion about Further Strengthening and Enhancing Dibao Implementation" issued by the State Council in 2012 stipulated less frequent verification of Dibao eligibility and benefit levels for Sanwu individuals (those without working ability, income source, or family support) and those foreseeing no significant income changes, most likely due to old age, poor health, childcare responsibilities, or other restrictions on employability. This, in effect, takes into consideration the healthcare, education, and other needs of these families in the determination of their Dibao eligibility and benefit levels. At the local level, as discussed in Chapter 6, some localities adopted a higher income disregard for families with ill, disabled, or older members so that these families could have a greater chance of being eligible for Dibao. Others offered differentiated benefit levels to those with different work abilities, such as families with children, elders, and members with disability.

It is important to note that both Dibao assistance standards and means testing are determined based on income rather than consumption. As many scholars argue that consumption is often a more accurate measure of family living standards and well-being, especially among the poor, it is appropriate to consider revising Dibao benefits based on consumption needs instead of income.

As findings reported in this chapter show, such a shift is not only necessary but urgent to ensure that Dibao achieves its anti-poverty goals and functions as a sufficient safety net for the poor.

To achieve these goals requires a fundamental shift in how we view what constitutes basic human needs (Dover & Joseph, 2008). Healthcare and education should be considered core livelihood elements in the policy design of Dibao. The adjustment of the Dibao line over the years mainly tried to keep pace with inflation rather than taking into consideration the specific consumption demands for healthcare, education, and other human needs. In both the policy design and implementation, unmet needs are often considered to be personal deficits and are stigmatized, rather than recognized as legitimate and dignified. It is important to shift this values system on which Dibao was envisioned and established so that all human needs can be met and Dibao can truly become an effective anti-poverty tool.

From a research perspective, it is important to bear in mind that most of the evidence presented in this chapter is descriptive or associational in nature. While the propensity score matching (PSM) method used in the several main studies helps us gain a more accurate estimate of the possible effects of Dibao receipt on family expenditures than otherwise possible, it can only take into account factors observable in the data and thus cannot eliminate the potential influence of any unobservable characteristics. Therefore, even though the results reported in this chapter are robust across various studies and in multiple sensitivity tests, they need to be interpreted with caution. For example, it is likely that corruption and favoritism by local officials who implement the Dibao program play a role in determining who among the poor becomes a recipient and who does not; this factor, unfortunately, is often immeasurable and unaccounted for in empirical analysis. Existing evidence indeed suggests the existence of such influence (Golan et al., 2014; Solinger, 2011), but there is no consensus on or generalizable estimate about the breadth or depth of such corruption and favoritism in Dibao implementation. Future research using multiple methods, both quantitative and qualitative, can help better understand the robustness and dynamics of these results and enable us to draw more solid policy implications. More rigorous research designs and longitudinal data collection efforts with a focus on low-income populations can help assess the causal and long-term effects of Dibao receipt on family expenditures and other outcomes.

8

SOCIAL PARTICIPATION AND
SUBJECTIVE WELL-BEING

As a means-tested cash transfer program, the goal of Dibao is to provide the necessary financial resources for poor families to maintain the minimum level of livelihood. Like most unconditional cash transfer (UCT) programs around the world, Dibao, for the most part, does not require certain behavioral changes from the recipients, nor does it seem to concern such behavioral reactions. However, as documented by the international literature, welfare programs similar to Dibao have had many behavioral responses from recipients, some intended but many others unintended. These behavioral outcomes are important, as they reflect recipients' direct reactions induced by such policies and programs and capture the longer-term effects of welfare participation.

As discussed in earlier chapters, most existing research on Dibao focuses on its monetary and material outcomes, such as poverty, income, and consumption. Very few empirical studies have examined how Dibao might be associated with recipients' behaviors, such as time use patterns and social participation, and subjective well-being, such as feelings of stigma, optimism, happiness, and overall quality of life. These outcomes are important, especially if policymakers and scholars view welfare recipients as integral and equal members of society instead of as a marginal and often less dignified subset of society. Providing rigorous evidence on this topic is especially challenging in China given the lack of longitudinal and experimental or quasi-experimental data.

In this chapter, I draw on the international literature on behavioral and subjective responses to welfare and summarize the limited evidence on how receiving Dibao might be associated with time use, social participation, and subjective well-being. This set of evidence sheds light on the complexity of welfare programs and their potential psychosocial influences, in addition to the much more

114

examined economic consequences. It offers important policy and research implications for Dibao's future design and implementation.

BEHAVIORAL RESPONSES TO WELFARE

The international literature has documented various behavioral responses to welfare participation. Most UCT programs like Dibao use strict means testing to determine welfare eligibility and then provide cash transfers to support livelihood. Their behavioral consequences are often unintended or unexpected. As discussed in Chapter 6, welfare receipt may discourage work efforts, especially at the margins of the eligibility threshold, where any additional earned income would mean the same amount being deducted from cash transfers. In countries where welfare benefits mainly target single-parent families, it is possible that UCT programs may discourage marriage but instead encourage cohabitation among couples.

Evidence from research on the Earned Income Tax Credit (EITC), the largest means-tested UCT program in the United States, suggests that the EITC has had a strong positive effect on labor force participation of single-mother households but a slight negative effect on the employment of married women. Despite some speculations about how the EITC might discourage marriage because of its much higher threshold for benefit eligibility for married couples, the empirical evidence has offered little evidence to support this claim (Hotz & Scholz, 2003; Hoynes, 2014; Meyer, 2010). Research has also shown the EITC to have positive effects on child health, school achievement, and college attendance (Dahl & Lochner, 2012; Evans & Garthwaite, 2014; Maxfield, 2013; Nichols & Rothstein, 2016). The other main UCT program in the United States, Temporary Assistance to Needy Families (TANF), has helped increase employment and earnings of low-income single-parent households, but its effects on marriage and non-marital childbirth are weak and mixed in the literature (Blank, 2009; Moffitt, 2003a; Ziliak, 2016).

Different from UCTs, conditional cash transfer (CCT) programs require certain behaviors as a condition for receiving cash transfers in addition to meeting the means-testing standard. These required actions often concentrate on human development activities such as school enrollment for children and regular doctor's visits. The economic and behavioral outcomes of many CCT programs have been evaluated through experimental or quasi-experimental studies, most notably randomized controlled trials (RCTs). The evidence regarding CCT programs shows clear positive effects on poverty reduction as well as increased school enrollment, improved preventive healthcare, and greater household consumption, especially spending on more nutritious food (Rawlings & Rubio, 2005; Soares, Ribas, & Osório, 2010).

Despite the growing body of international literature on the effects of welfare on behavioral outcomes, the possible link between welfare participation and recipient time use and social participation patterns has not been much explored. Given the social-labeling effect of being a welfare recipient, especially the strong stigma associated with UCT programs, it is important to understand whether receiving welfare discourages social participation and induces a less active life. Further, subjective well-being has become an increasingly important indicator of people's living conditions and overall quality of life (e.g., Appleton & Song, 2008; Brockmann, Delhey, Welzel, & Yuan, 2009; Cheung & Leung, 2004; Easterlin, 2001; Frey & Stutzer, 2002; Huang, Wu, & Deng, 2015; Layard, 2005; Smyth, Nielsen, & Zhai, 2010). Welfare recipients may be happier because of the higher income from cash transfers, but the stigma associated with receiving benefits could be demoralizing and damage their subjective well-being. These understudied aspects deserve more attention from researchers and policymakers and are becoming more prominent in global policy discussions.

TIME USE AND SOCIAL PARTICIPATION

Among the possible behavioral responses to welfare participation, time use is arguably the most accurate reflection of how people might react to receiving welfare benefits. A surge of time use surveys across countries during recent years has helped promote much-needed research on people's time use patterns and how such patterns are affected by various factors (Harvey, 2004). While the body of research on time use in general has been growing worldwide, the possible link between welfare participation and time use has rarely been empirically explored.

Using the China Family Panel Studies (CFPS) 2010 survey data and a propensity score matching (PSM) method, my colleagues and I (Gao, Wu, & Zhai, 2015) examined the association between welfare participation and household heads' time use patterns in both urban and rural areas. We found that both urban and rural Dibao receipt was associated with less time spent on leisure and social activities and more time spent on non-specified activities or being idle, a possibly unintended adverse effect of this safety net program. Dibao was also associated with less time spent on education activities for urban recipients and less time spent on work activities but more time on personal and household care activities for rural recipients.

Specifically, as shown in Figure 8.1, the most notable finding was the consistent negative association between Dibao receipt and time spent on leisure and social activities across urban and rural areas on both work and non-work days. Urban Dibao recipients decreased their time spent on leisure and social activities by 0.52 hours (i.e., 31 minutes) on a typical work day and 0.77 hours (i.e., 46 minutes) on a typical non-work day. Rural Dibao recipients reduced their leisure and social activity time by 0.42 hours (i.e., 25 minutes) and 0.47 hours (i.e., 28 minutes) on respective work and non-work days. This is most likely because Dibao recipients were afraid of being seen as indulging and not hard-working and thus

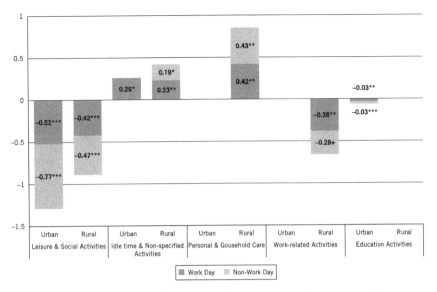

Figure 8.1. Association between Dibao receipt and time use patterns (hours/day). *** *p* < 0.001, ** *p* < 0.01, * *p* < 0.05, + *p* < 0.10. Source: Gao, Wu, and Zhai (2015), using China Family Panel Studies (CFPS) 2010 survey data.

non-deserving of welfare benefits. This is a realistic concern, as Dibao eligibility is reassessed every 3 to 6 months through means testing and public monitoring, so a neighbor or community member could raise concerns about the eligibility of certain Dibao recipients if some of their activities appear suspicious and too indulging.

What specific leisure and social activities did Dibao recipients spend less time on as compared to their non-recipient peers? Figure 8.2 presents the magnitude of significant associations between Dibao receipt and time spent on specific leisure and social activities. Among the activities of a socializing or public nature, for both urban and rural recipients, Dibao receipt was associated with less time spent on participating in recreational activities, such as playing games with others and using the Internet. Urban recipients also reduced their time spent on exercising, while rural recipients decreased their time spent on social activities.

Research based on qualitative interviews and fieldwork support these findings. For example, Solinger (2012) found that most Dibao recipients felt ashamed to associate with neighbors, former colleagues, and even extended family members. One Dibao recipient in Beijing, in a 2007 in-depth interview, said, "Me still having social activities?! Still hanging out with friends? Basically none! If someone comes to visit, then we figure something out at home. Basically I have no social activities these days" (Han, 2012, p. 51; interviewee: 46-year-old Mr. Wang).

Figure 8.2 also shows that, among the leisure activities that are more private, Dibao was associated with reduced time spent watching TV and listening to the

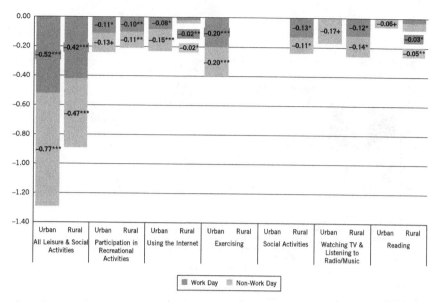

Figure 8.2. Association between Dibao receipt and time spent on leisure and social activities (hours/day). *** $p < 0.001$, ** $p < 0.01$, * $p < 0.05$, + $p < 0.10$. Source: Gao, Wu, and Zhai (2015), using China Family Panel Studies (CFPS) 2010 survey data.

radio or music as well as reading for both urban and rural recipients. Specifically, urban Dibao recipients reduced their time spent watching TV and listening to the radio or music by 10 minutes on typical non-work days, while rural Dibao recipients decreased their time spent on the same activities by 7 to 8 minutes on both work and non-work days. Similarly, Dibao receipt was associated with less time spent on reading for both urban and rural residents, although only by 2 to 4 minutes per day. These negative associations between Dibao receipt and leisure activities in private may be due to the demoralizing Dibao application and means-testing process, but they may also manifest pre-existing differences in social isolation between Dibao recipients and non-recipients, which the PSM method cannot capture.

Parallel to the negative findings on leisure and social activities, Figure 8.1 further shows that both urban and rural Dibao receipt were associated with increased time spent on non-specified activities or being idle, inferring an unfortunate state of boredom or meaninglessness. Specifically, urban Dibao recipients tended to increase their idle time by 0.26 hours (i.e., 16 minutes) on a typical work day, while rural Dibao recipients tended to increase their time spent on non-specified activities by 0.23 hours (i.e., 14 minutes) on a typical work day and 0.19 hours (i.e., 11 minutes) on a typical non-work day.

There seemed to be additional possible adverse effects of Dibao for both urban and rural recipients. Specifically, rural Dibao receipt was associated with more time spent on personal and household care activities by about 0.42 hours (i.e., 25 minutes) on both work and non-work days, which means extra time spent alone and avoiding the public. Not shown in Figure 8.1 but as reported by Gao, Wu, and Zhai (2015), much of this additional time was spent on housekeeping (0.27 hours, or 16 minutes, on both work and non-work days) and sleeping and resting (0.16 hours, or 10 minutes, on work days and 0.23 hours, or 14 minutes, on non-work days).

Figure 8.1 also shows that Dibao receipt was associated with decreased time spent on work activities in rural areas and less time spent on educational activities in urban areas, echoing the discussion in Chapter 6 about how Dibao might deter recipients from working and encourage welfare dependency. Specifically, rural Dibao recipients reduced their time spent on work-related activities by 0.38 hours (i.e., 23 minutes) on work days and 0.28 hours (i.e., 17 minutes) on non-work days. Urban Dibao recipients reduced their time spent on educational activities slightly by 0.03 hours (i.e., 2 minutes) on both work and non-work days.

These findings suggest that Dibao is associated with reduced leisure and social activities. Further analysis of the CFPS 2010 data show that Dibao receipt was associated with reduced frequencies of leisure activities of a socializing nature as well as religious activities (Gao & Wang, 2016). Specifically, as shown in Figure 8.3 in both urban and rural areas, Dibao receipt was associated with less travel. Among rural recipients, Dibao was associated with fewer religious activities. Among urban recipients, Dibao was associated with less exercising, dining out, and playing cards with others, a popular game played in groups among neighbors and friends. As discussed in Chapter 7, analysis based on rural household

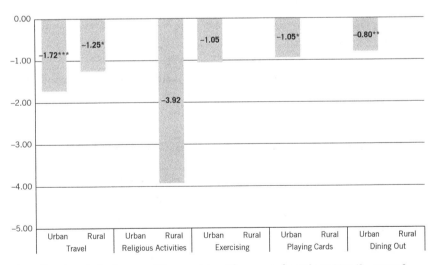

Figure 8.3. Association between Dibao receipt and frequency of social activities (0 = never; 1 = once every few months; 2 = once a month; 3 = several times a month; 4 = several times a week; 5 = almost every day). *** $p < 0.001$, ** $p < 0.01$, * $p < 0.05$, + $p < 0.10$. Source: Gao and Wang (2016), using China Family Panel Studies (CFPS) 2010 survey data.

survey data from five central and western provinces in 2010 also suggest that rural Dibao residents spent less money on items required for participating in social activities (Han et al., 2016).

STIGMA, SHAME, AND DESPAIR

Evidence across qualitative and quantitative studies shows that Dibao recipients as a group bear the strong stigma of being on welfare. Nearly all recipients in qualitative interviews mention how stigma affects their lives and express their shame and despair in receiving Dibao. Such evidence offers direct explanation for the reduced leisure activities and social participation among Dibao recipients documented earlier.

In both urban and rural areas, Dibao recipients appear to be more likely to be pessimistic about future prospects and unhappy about their life situation, possibly due to selection or disincentives induced by Dibao receipt or a combination of these two factors. Estimates based on CHIP 2002 urban data show that 25% of Dibao recipients believed that their income would decrease in the next 5 years as compared to 19% of non-recipients. Further, 36% of Dibao recipients felt unhappy about their life situation as compared to 12% of non-recipients. Estimates from the CFPS 2010 data show that 17% of urban Dibao recipients reported being unhappy and 29% reported being unsatisfied with life in general, as compared to 8% and 16% of non-recipients, respectively. Among rural recipients, 24% reported being unhappy and 26% reported being dissatisfied with life in general, as compared to 12% and 15% of non-recipients, respectively.

Many Dibao recipients interviewed by Solinger (2011, 2012) were so ashamed of their situation that they concealed the fact of their job loss from their acquaintances. In fact, detachment and loneliness were constant themes of multiple interviews. Solinger (2012) especially discovered the lack of communication, cooperation, and organization among Dibao recipients themselves, disputing the possibility of this group forming a distinctive class and having a shared class consciousness.

In the extensive interviews conducted by Han (2012) and his research team across six cities, nearly every Dibao recipient mentioned stigma and shame, especially when talking about their children. Many also expressed hopelessness and despair about the reality and future. For example, one Dibao recipient in Beijing said, "Life to me now is relatively bleak. I'm a little scared. Can only manage it day by day" (Han, 2012, p. 6; interviewee: 34-year-old Mr. Kong).

Another Dibao recipient in Beijing in the same study actually shielded the family's Dibao recipient status from his son because "we are afraid that other kids might laugh at him. Kids nowadays compare with each other. . . . We are afraid that he might have psychological burden" (Han, 2012, p. 50; interviewee: 46-year-old

Mr. Wang). For the same reason, he did not apply for reduced tuition for his son either.

A major reason for such shame and despair is the forced disclosure of privacy—in both financial and other family situations—to neighbors and the broader community. One Dibao recipient in Changsha who had gynecological disease shared her embarrassment of having to make her health conditions public: "My body is full of disease, but others do not know. They look at me, walking, standing, all fine, ah, you should be able to work.... Why would you rely on Dibao?" (Han, 2012, pp. 173–174; interviewee: 40-year-old Ms. Yang).

Some Dibao recipients also acknowledged support from others and some level of satisfaction and hope with life, adding some light to this generally dismal picture. For example, this same interviewee, Ms. Yang, mentioned kind invitations from neighbors to share a meal or special treats (Han, 2012, p. 172). However, given the day-to-day struggles and lack of better prospects, most Dibao recipients remain desperate and hopeless about the future. One Dibao recipient in Chaoyang city of Liaoning province said that she had "not a bit of hope for this world" when thinking about her husband who had multiple diseases and her daughter who was attending college and needed money for tuition (Han, 2012, p. 197; interviewee: 43-year-old Ms. Gao).

OUTLOOK AND SUBJECTIVE WELL-BEING

A growing set of studies has investigated the trends and determinants of subjective well-being in China (Appleton & Song, 2008; Brockmann et al., 2009; Cheung & Leung, 2004; Huang, Wu, et al., 2015; Knight & Gunatilaka, 2011; Smyth, Nielsen, & Zhai, 2010). They identified low income, unemployment, poor health, and lack of health insurance as the main predictors of low subjective well-being. As shown in Chapter 3, all of these risk factors are key characteristics of Dibao recipients, suggesting that Dibao receipt might be associated with low subjective well-being despite the income gain due to receiving this cash transfer.

Among these factors, economic well-being and prospects have been identified as the strongest predictor of subjective well-being and happiness. Using data from the Urban Household Short Survey (UHSS) for 2003–2004 collected in 35 large cities, Chen et al. (2006) found that 81% of Dibao recipients considered their income to be less than adequate for their needs, while only 30% of the overall urban population thought so, indicating lower perceived economic well-being among Dibao recipients than among their non-recipient peers.

Given the prevalence and depth of stigma, shame, and despair felt by so many Dibao recipients, is it possible for Dibao recipients to have greater subjective well-being than their equally poor non-recipient peers? As discussed earlier in Chapter 4, like many similar means-tested cash transfer programs,

Dibao has serious targeting errors, leaving many eligible families not covered by Dibao. From a research perspective, the eligible non-recipient group serves as the best available comparison group for Dibao recipients. Using a PSM method can help identify non-recipients who are similar to the recipients in observable demographic and socioeconomic characteristics. Granted, the matched groups may still have some differences in non-observable characteristics, but the comparisons based on the matched sample offer a much more accurate comparison between the two groups than otherwise possible. However, it is important to note that any matching method inherently relies on observable information in the data source and thus cannot fully rule out selection bias.

My colleagues and I (Gao, Wu, Wu, & Zhai, 2016; Gao & Zhai, 2015) used two different large data sets and a PSM method to understand the possible association between Dibao and recipients' subjective well-being. We found that Dibao receipt was associated with less happiness and satisfaction with life. Further, this negative association was mediated by Dibao recipients' dismal outlook for future income and perceived social class.

Specifically, using CHIP 2002 urban data, Gao and Zhai (2015) found that, compared to their matched non-recipient peers, Dibao recipients were more likely to believe that they would have no increase in income over the next 5 years (by 38%) and that the societal income distribution was unfair (by 189%), and in general had greater odds of feeling unhappy (by 128%). In particular, the projected lack of increase of income over the next 5 years was significantly associated with unhappiness even after Dibao receipt status was taken into account. This suggests that the prospect of low income was the main concern of the Dibao recipients.

We used mediation analysis to further understand the possible associational pathways among Dibao receipt, income prospect, and unhappiness. This analysis showed that the projected lack of income increase in the next 5 years accounted for 8% of Dibao's association with reduced happiness, indicating that Dibao receipt itself and the associated stigma and shame of being on welfare still had a strong direct influence on recipients' degree of happiness.

Using the CFPS 2010 data, my colleagues and I (Gao, Wu et al., 2016) further found that, in both urban and rural areas, Dibao receipt was associated with a lower level of happiness. For urban recipients, Dibao was also associated with lower levels of overall life satisfaction. We also found that recipients' perceived social class as measured by self-reported social status in the local context, ranging from very low to very high, significantly mediated the association between Dibao receipt and happiness as well as life satisfaction. In both urban and rural areas, perceived social class accounted for 20% of Dibao's association with happiness. Perceived social class accounted for 27% of Dibao's association with life satisfaction for urban recipients and 54% of the association for rural recipients, manifesting the more predominant influence of community and social status among rural residents than among their urban peers.

SUMMARY AND IMPLICATIONS

This chapter documents Dibao's possible negative influence on behavioral and subjective outcomes for both urban and rural recipients. Evidence from qualitative and quantitative studies shows that Dibao recipients live a more isolated and detached life and engage in fewer leisure and social activities than their non-recipient peers. The stigma, shame, and despair associated with receiving Dibao are also linked to a poor outlook for income and social class as well as low levels of happiness and life satisfaction. In addition, there is some evidence that Dibao receipt is associated with less time spent on education and work activities, echoing the many challenges faced by Dibao recipients to move from welfare to work, discussed in Chapter 6.

These findings offer important insights into the non-economic aspects of Dibao recipients' lives and provide timely policy implications. As a means-tested cash transfer program, Dibao's primary goal is to serve as a last-resort safety net for the very poor by providing a minimum amount of necessary resources. However, it is important for policymakers to monitor the possible behavioral and subjective consequences of being a welfare recipient, especially when these consequences are unintended and negative.

From a policy perspective, some important changes can be made to the design and implementation of Dibao to address these adverse consequences. First and foremost, the strong stigma associated with receiving Dibao is most prominent in the benefit application and approval process. Dibao recipients have to obtain multiple certificates from their local residential committees, former or current employers, and children's schools to prove their lack of income and need for support. This lengthy process is coupled with the public display of their names on community bulletin boards for scrutiny and feedback from neighbors and other community members. Further, children from Dibao families are often clearly labeled in their schools. All of these make Dibao recipients feel ashamed, which may lead them to partake in fewer leisure and social activities and feel more unhappy and hopeless about the future.

It is important to modify some of these means-testing procedures and approaches so that Dibao recipients can maintain some privacy and dignity and suffer less from stigma and public pressure. Such a change may also help encourage Dibao recipients to participate in more education, work, and social activities and become more engaging and contributing members of the society. For Dibao children, it is important that they have dignity among their peers and work hard so that there is hope for breaking free from the intergenerational poverty trap.

Second, the perceived lack of income increase and low social class among Dibao recipients are alarming. It is important to establish and strengthen work support programs to enable Dibao recipients to move from welfare to work, as discussed in Chapter 6. It is also important to adjust the Dibao assistance standards so that they truly keep pace with inflation and the average living standard, as discussed in Chapter 3.

Third, as is evident from the qualitative evidence cited in this chapter, the despair felt by many Dibao recipients is due to extra burden from healthcare and education needs, which are not sufficiently addressed by Dibao or its supplementary programs. For families with these needs, especially education support for children, it is important to broaden support from both Dibao and its supplementary programs so that sufficient resources are provided to cover these demands. As discussed in Chapter 7, they should be considered basic human needs and essential elements for a dignified and fulfilled life.

From a research perspective, it is important to be fully aware of the associational rather than causal nature of the findings presented in this chapter. Most existing studies use cross-sectional, observational survey data and thus lack the rigor of experimental or quasi-experimental research. Using matching methods such as PSM helps remove some selection bias but cannot eliminate it entirely. Thus, it is an empirical question whether the findings of this set of studies are due to selection or disincentives induced by Dibao receipt. Future research needs to use more rigorous designs and methodologies to address this question and tease out the causal effect of Dibao receipt on behavioral and subjective outcomes.

It is also important to develop surveys that incorporate important behavioral and subjective measures into Dibao research. Without such measures, researchers would not be able to monitor the possible behavioral and subjective responses to Dibao. Time use data and measures of subjective well-being, two rapidly growing research areas internationally, are especially important to be considered as integral parts of welfare research. Given the long-term nature of these outcomes, it is important to carry out longitudinal surveys to enable the tracking of these measures over time. It is possible that many such behavioral and subjective responses would affect the development trajectories and mental health of children in Dibao families. Only longitudinal studies with repeated measures can help capture these long-term effects and offer appropriate policy implications. The Chinese evidence on this large cash transfer program will undoubtedly enrich the global literature and help provide solutions for addressing these adverse effects in similar welfare programs worldwide.

9

WHAT NEXT? POLICY SOLUTIONS AND RESEARCH DIRECTIONS

Based on the extensive review of policy trends and empirical evidence on Dibao's impact and effectiveness, in this chapter, I propose policy solutions to help improve the performance of Dibao in the future. I also highlight research directions that can help further the monitoring and evaluation of Dibao's performance.

POLICY SOLUTIONS

From a policy perspective, Dibao's performance can be improved in three aspects: its design, its implementation, and its coordination with other social welfare programs and fit within the broader social benefit system.

Focusing on Dibao's *policy design*, first and foremost, it is important to recognize that the current Dibao assistance standards are set at very low levels, especially relative to average income and consumption levels as well as the pace of increases in consumer prices, despite their annual increases in nominal terms. As shown in the evidence presented in earlier chapters, such limited benefit generosity may be insufficient to meet even the basic survival needs of recipient families. Moving forward, it is important to reconsider what constitutes "minimum livelihood" to be supported by Dibao, reassess the sufficiency of the Dibao lines across localities, and raise these lines so that they can truly serve as a last-resort safety net for the most disadvantaged in both rural and urban areas of China.

One core requirement for this exercise is the reconsideration of what constitutes "minimum livelihood" or "basic human needs" (Dover & Joseph, 2008). The current policy design of Dibao considers essential material goods, including food, clothing, and shelter, as basic needs while taking into consideration utility, medical care, and tuition expenses. However, healthcare and education are seen as secondary, nonessential needs, even though they constitute the majority of Dibao families' expenses, as is evident in Chapter 7. Given the overwhelming importance of health and education for livelihood and life opportunities in today's society, it is necessary to have a shift in values that considers these two items as part of basic livelihood and includes them in setting the Dibao lines and benefit levels. It is promising that both national regulations and local experimentations have recognized this need and are moving in this direction. However, it takes determination and continued efforts to accomplish this shift across localities and to incorporate it into Dibao's policy design in the long term.

Another aspect of human needs that deserves consideration is cultural and spiritual needs that some Dibao recipients long for, especially given their isolation due to limited social activities and narrow social networks. For example, some Dibao recipients have suggested the possibility of receiving vouchers or low-cost tickets to parks and museums, especially for their children, so that they could enjoy some outings and enrichment (Han, 2012). Such programs exist in many developed countries, to encourage exposure to enrichment programs for children and personal fulfillment among adults from low-income families. Such programs may serve as one important channel for breaking the intergenerational transmission of poverty.

Second, it is also important to have built-in flexibility to consider individual and family circumstances when determining the Dibao lines and benefit levels. As documented in several earlier chapters, many Dibao families face unique challenges, such as serious or chronic disease, mental illness, family care responsibilities, and limited education and skills, that restrict their participation in the labor market and their prospects for work. Many have no choice but to rely on welfare, despite their reluctance and shame at being dependent on welfare. Even though the current regulations allow some leeway for considering these factors, these families are mostly treated the same as other applicants, and their eligibility and benefit levels are determined on the basis of income and assets as well as Hukou status like everyone else. Applying the same standards to families with these special needs may be inadequate to support them in managing livelihood and moving toward self-sufficiency.

In the context of reconsidering what constitutes basic human needs and having built-in flexibility in determining Dibao lines and benefit levels, the central government's recent initiative to standardize the approaches used by local governments to set their Dibao lines may work as a double-edged sword. On the one hand, it can bring some clarity and consistency to the methods used for setting local Dibao lines. On the other hand, it could deprive local governments of their freedom and autonomy in applying the most appropriate and effective approaches for identifying and supporting Dibao families in the local context, which may make the program unnecessarily rigid and less efficient. Given that most local officials rely on the central evaluation system for their performance assessment and promotion, it is most likely that they will oblige these new regulations to follow the central guidelines and sacrifice some local autonomy and creativity. The influence of this set of new regulations needs to be closely monitored and evaluated.

Third, Dibao's population coverage has been shrinking in recent years, especially in urban areas, covering only 2.5% of the urban population in 2014. Its growth in population coverage in rural areas also slowed during 2010–2013 and had a significant drop from 2013 to 2014. Such a trend corresponds to the central government's recent shift to emphasize Dibao recipients' work efforts and focus on the most disadvantaged rather than those who are deemed less deserving (Solinger, 2015b). However, international evidence suggests that narrower population coverage usually leads to less poverty reduction. As China's primary public assistance program, Dibao's modest anti-poverty effectiveness would certainly suffer further because of this narrower population coverage, an unfortunate and probably unintended outcome. It is important to keep this consequence in mind and to broaden Dibao's population coverage in order to maintain and improve its poverty reduction effects.

Fourth, as a strict means-testing program, Dibao's eligibility screening process is very demeaning and stigmatizing, in effect deterring many potentially eligible individuals and families from applying for Dibao and shaming those who receive benefits into becoming a socially marginalized and excluded group. It is a delicate act to balance means testing and human dignity. Most similar welfare programs around the world face this same challenge, but few adopt a screening procedure that involves as extensive public scrutiny and humiliation as Dibao does. This is partly because of the existence of reliable information systems on income and taxes in most developed countries (such as the United States) and some developing countries (such as Brazil), which makes extensive, intrusive means testing unnecessary, and partly because of China's tradition of community involvement and disregard for individual and family privacy since the establishment of the communist regime. As China moves toward a more market-oriented, more democratic society, it is important to gradually shift this stigmatizing, marginalizing approach to a more respectful, inclusive approach of means testing. Such a transition can also help ensure better targeting performance and greater anti-poverty effectiveness of Dibao, as more eligible families would apply for benefits and recipient families might be more motivated to move from welfare to work and be an active, integral part of society.

With regard to Dibao's *implementation*, first, given the high leakage and mistargeting rates in Dibao's performance, it is important to provide accurate and timely public information and education about Dibao eligibility, application and screening procedures, and monitoring and evaluation process. This will help encourage the truly eligible to apply and ensure that Dibao reaches its target population for maximized utility. It will also help deter inefficiency and corruption and enhance the effectiveness and efficiency of public involvement and monitoring of Dibao performance.

Second, it is important to build a more professional team of Dibao administrators who are not only familiar with Dibao's implementation procedures but also understanding, empathetic, respectful, and efficient in their attitudes toward Dibao applicants and beneficiaries. These administrators should also be resourceful, having full knowledge of the existence of other support systems beyond Dibao, and be able to provide referrals for necessary benefits and services efficiently.

Third, thus far, Dibao's implementation has relied on the government system but lacked involvement and collaboration with the non-governmental sector. The main strengths of the government system are its ubiquitous horizontal and vertical branches with far reach and its long history of administering similar programs. The main limitations of the government system are its prioritizing of political objectives and regulations over the goals of the Dibao program and the well-being of Dibao's target population. Experiences from around the world have showcased the power of building effective collaborations with the non-governmental sector, with the government providing basic regulations and the majority of funding but entrusting the non-governmental organizations (NGOs) with the details of implementation as well as room for creativity and innovation. As China's non-governmental sector grows, such collaboration could work to streamline the Dibao screening and benefit delivery system for the government and enhance its efficiency and effectiveness.

Dibao's performance can also be improved by *better coordination with other social welfare programs and fit within the broader social benefit system*. As shown in earlier chapters, many Dibao families are in desperate need of education and healthcare support. As a result, they tend to prioritize using their Dibao benefits to pay for education and healthcare and thus sacrifice meeting basic survival needs, such as food, clothing, and utilities. This highlights the lack of a sufficient education and healthcare support system for the poor. To address such gaps, first, the current education and health assistance programs need to be broadened to cover all of those in need. Their benefit levels should also be improved so that the beneficiaries' education and healthcare needs can be fully met through these programs and Dibao can be used for basic survival needs. Education assistance is especially important for supporting families with children enrolled in high school or higher education, both of which are noncompulsory and involve high costs.

Second and more important, the compulsory education system needs to be strengthened so that it is truly compulsory and families do not have to pay extra fees to obtain basic education. This is especially important in less developed regions and rural areas, where local investments in education tend to be lagging and insufficient. Coupled with fewer education investments in these localities are low quality of education and high family expenses for education. Such unbalanced conditions need to be fixed so that all children can receive free, good-quality compulsory education, regardless of family background or residential location. Rural-to-urban migrant children, who often cannot access the urban education system, should be included and treated equally. Only through such broad and equal investments in education can the next generation of Chinese citizens achieve their full potential and help the country stay competitive in the global environment.

Third, the fragmented health insurance system in China needs to be unified and balanced so that rural residents and the unemployed in urban areas can have broader coverage and more comprehensive benefits to meet their healthcare needs. The current health insurance system is stratified so that urban employees, especially public servants, have substantially better healthcare coverage than their unemployed urban peers and rural residents. The new resident health insurance schemes have been helpful in providing coverage for these two groups, but their premium levels can be high relative to their low income levels, especially among the poor, and their coverage remains narrow and benefit levels remain low (Duckett, 2011; Huang, 2015; Huang & Gao, 2015). Only through a true unification and equity-oriented approach can the health insurance system be broadened to cover all Chinese citizens and ensure that the poor are not left behind by the system.

Fourth, in addition to education and healthcare, it is important to expand the social insurance system, especially pensions but also unemployment and work injury insurances, for the poor. As shown in Chapter 7, it is nearly impossible for Dibao recipients to afford contributions to social insurance, which in turn leads to the lack of long-term social protection and prolonged welfare dependency for this group. In the United States, Supplemental Security Income (SSI) provides monthly federal cash assistance to low-income individuals who are either elderly (65 or older), blind, or disabled. Most states also allow SSI recipients to have concurrent access to Medicaid, a government health insurance program for low-income persons, and sometimes housing benefits. These benefits serve as an important means of supporting the various aspects of low-income families' livelihood and enable individuals from these families to pursue education and job opportunities.

Another important gap to consider is the ineffectiveness of current work support programs to help facilitate and promote the transition from welfare to work. As shown in Chapter 6, many localities have experimented with various welfare-to-work initiatives, but few have shown to be effective and most have not been systematically evaluated for effectiveness. Going forward, it is important to move from demeaning, punitive approaches to more effective, protective, and encouraging approaches of work support programs. The design and implementation of such programs should take into consideration not only broad labor market trends but also Dibao families' specific circumstances so that any initiatives would address their needs and help them move from welfare to work effectively.

Any continuing or new work support programs also need to be closely monitored and evaluated in order to provide implications for future directions.

Building a broader social benefit system also involves providing community resources and social services to support poor families to not only manage their basic livelihood but also meet their family care and social participation needs. Globally, there is a greater demand to value care as much as work activities (Slaughter, 2015). Evidence presented in this book shows that many Dibao families have to juggle multiple demands of family and healthcare, on top of struggling to survive. The lack of community resources offering childcare and senior care services adds to the burden shouldered by these families. In a recent demonstration project, the Ministry of Civil Affairs (MCA), in collaboration with the Asian Development Bank (ADB), has explored possible approaches to combining social assistance and professional social services effectively to better meet the needs of low-income families. As the social work profession continues to grow and expand in China, such a combination would benefit not only the Dibao population but also the broader society to build stronger, more inclusive and cohesive communities and social networks.

In sum, as the Chinese government works to build a unified social welfare system, especially a strong social insurance system for urban and rural residents, it is important that Dibao functions as an integral and effective social assistance program to support those left behind by both the market and the social welfare system. In particular, Dibao needs to improve its design and implementation to enhance its targeting performance, population coverage, benefit delivery, and anti-poverty effectiveness. Meanwhile, other programs, such as education, healthcare, social insurances, and work support, need to be strengthened in order to stimulate greater human capital investment and improve both material and subjective well-being of Dibao's target population.

RESEARCH DIRECTIONS

A growing body of international literature has focused on the monitoring and evaluation of welfare programs, including both conditional and unconditional cash transfer programs such as Dibao. In the Chinese context, this book offers the first thorough examination of Dibao's impact and effectiveness on multidimensional outcomes. Based on the lessons learned through this book, I propose the following research directions that could help improve the monitoring and evaluation of Dibao's performance in the future.

First and foremost, based on lessons from other countries as well as from the existing evidence on Dibao, we need to design and carry out more rigorous, better coordinated longitudinal research studies focusing on Dibao's target population (including the near-poor as a comparison group as well as potential Dibao beneficiaries) and multidimensional outcomes. The lack of such data limits the ability for testing the causal effects of Dibao and drawing direct policy implications. For example, one key challenge faced by many empirical studies reviewed in this book is whether certain outcomes, such as increased human capital investment and reduced social participation, is due to Dibao receipt or selection bias. It is nearly impossible to tackle this difficult question without more rigorous research designs, such as experiments or longitudinal data. As Barrientos (2013) pointed out, very few developing or transitional countries have longitudinal data sets suitable for the evaluation of the causal effects of welfare programs. As data collection efforts in China continue to grow, researchers and policymakers need to use more rigorous designs and collect longitudinal data to reach more robust conclusions and provide more sound policy implications for Dibao and other welfare programs.

It is also important to use multiple data sources at both the national and subnational level to replicate and verify evaluation findings of Dibao. Internationally, replication research has been a growing trend in firmly establishing the impacts of social welfare programs and offering specific policy implications (Brown, Cameron, & Wood, 2014). Replication research is especially important for understanding and establishing the causal effects of Dibao, given its urban–rural difference and decentralized implementation.

Second, it is important to examine multidimensional outcomes beyond targeting, poverty, income, and family consumption. Social assistance programs have profound and long-term impacts on participating families. Potential outcomes include but are not limited to (1) multidimensional poverty, including material deprivation and hardships; (2) human development, with a particular focus on education, health, and life opportunities; (3) likelihood for breaking the intergenerational transmission of poverty; (4) moving from welfare to work and self-sufficiency; and (5) other behavioral and subjective outcomes, such as social participation, self-esteem, optimism, and overall quality of life.

Third, future evaluations of Dibao should have a particular focus on children. If there is one lesson we can learn from successful conditional cash transfer (CCT) programs around the world, it is that focusing on children's human development leads to poverty reduction. The international literature has documented the wide and persistent existence of the trap of intergenerational poverty, which severely limits life opportunities of children from poor families. Dibao evaluation and implementation in the future should focus on investing in children's human capital and their long-term developmental outcomes. Only through improved human capital and life opportunities can children from poor families gain a less dismal future and have their fair chance for success in society.

Fourth, particular attention needs to be paid to Dibao's localized implementation in its monitoring and evaluation. Dibao is a national policy, but its assistance standards and implementation are very decentralized, with substantial variations across localities. It is important to carry out close monitoring and rigorous evaluations of selected, representative local Dibao programs to offer insights into what works, what does not work, and what can work better in the future. On this point, evaluation of the Temporary Assistance to Needy Families (TANF) in the United States can serve as a good example. It is similarly decentralized at the state level, and many states have collaborated with research teams to carry out demonstration and evaluation projects, which have provided ample research evidence to help improve its effectiveness locally and nationally. Similar work can be done for Dibao, involving local governments and research teams but with national and international collaboration, oversight, and collective expertise.

Finally, joint efforts should be made among interdisciplinary scholars, government officials, and international organizations to improve the monitoring and evaluation of Dibao. Dibao monitoring and evaluation can benefit greatly from coordinated joint efforts among all who care about Dibao and wish to improve it. International organizations such as the World Bank, ADB, and UNICEF have all worked toward this direction in collaboration with the Chinese government as well as research scholars. A more coordinated team effort will help provide a breakthrough in Dibao research and place the Chinese social assistance case more prominently in the global dialogue on welfare, work, and poverty.

ACKNOWLEDGMENTS

Writing this book has been an enormously rewarding experience. I owe thanks to many who offered help, support, and encouragement during the process. For helpful comments and suggestions, I thank Enid Opal Cox, Mark Frazier, Irv Garfinkel, Neil Gilbert, Jing Guo, Björn Gustafsson, Carl Riskin, Dorothy Solinger, Fuhua Zhai, Fenghua Zhou, and several anonymous reviewers. Xitang Liu, the Director of the Department of Social Assistance of China's Ministry of Civil Affairs, generously answered questions and shared insights. Part of the book was written while I was serving as a consultant for the World Bank Project on Monitoring and Evaluation of Social Assistance in China. I am thankful for discussions with Dewen Wang, the project task team leader, which benefited the book. As part of my participation in the National Committee on United States-China Relations Public Intellectuals Program, I presented this book to my peer public intellectuals and benefited from their feedback and encouragement.

For valuable encouragement and support, I am grateful to Roslyn Chernesky, Marlene Cooper, Carole Cox, Enid Opal Cox, Maddy and Hugh Cunningham, Bernie Gorman, Xinping Guan, Sheila Kamerman, Carol and Larry Kaplan, Winnie Kung, Shi Li, Xiaofang Liu, Brenda McGowan, Debra McPhee, Andy Nathan, Manoj Pardasani, Howard and Roberta Robinson, Terry Sicular, Judy Smith, Jeanette Takamura, Peter and Patricia Vaughan, Jane Waldfogel, Sibin Wang, Yuebin Xu, Dali L. Yang, and Rong Yang. For outstanding research assistance, I thank Xiaoran Wang, Sui Yang, Yu Yang, and Yalu Zhang. I am also grateful to my editors at Oxford University Press, Dana Bliss, Andrew Dominello, and Stefano Imbert, and the co-editors of the Series on Comparative Policy Analysis,

Neil Gilbert and Douglas Besharov. They have been most supportive during this process.

I thank two publishers who have granted me permission to use selected texts from articles that I published in peer-reviewed journals. They are Elsevier (publisher of *The Quarterly Review of Economics and Finance* and *World Development*) and John Wiley and Sons (publisher of *Review of Income and Wealth*).

This book is not possible without the steady support of my family. To Fuhua, Kevin, and Kenneth: thank you for your love, support, encouragement, and companionship, all of which sustained me and gave me courage and perseverance to complete this project. My parents and siblings offered support and encouragement throughout the process. This book is written in memory of my grandparents and dedicated to my parents. What they taught me about compassion, hard work, and dignity continues to be the pillars of my research and life. For this, I am forever grateful.

REFERENCES

Aizer, A., Eli, S., Ferrie, J., & Lleras-Muney, A. (2014). *The long term impact of cash transfers to poor families* (Working Paper No. 20103). Cambridge, MA: The National Bureau of Economic Research. Retrieved from http://www.nber.org/papers/w20103

Appleton, S., & Song, L. (2008). Life satisfaction in urban China: Components and determinants. *World Development, 36*(11), 2325–2340.

Asian Development Bank [ADB]. (2009). *The People's Republic of China: Updating and improving the Social Protection Index.* Manila: Asian Development Bank.

Attanasio, O., & Kaufmann, K. (2014). Education choices and returns to schooling: Mothers' and youths' subjective expectations and their role by gender. *Journal of Development Economics, 109*, 203–216.

Attanasio, O., & Mesnard, A. (2006). The impact of a conditional cash transfer program on consumption in Colombia. *Fiscal Studies, 27*(4), 421–442.

Baird, S., Ferreira, F., Özler, B., & Woolcock, M. (2014). Conditional, unconditional and everything in between: A systematic review of the effects of cash transfer programmes on schooling outcomes. *Journal of Development Effectiveness, 6*(1), 1–43.

Baird, S., McIntosh, C., & Özler, B. (2011). Cash or condition? Evidence from a cash transfer experiment. *The Quarterly Journal of Economics, 126*(4), 1–44.

Barrientos, A. (2013). *Social assistance in developing countries.* Cambridge, UK: Cambridge University Press.

Barrientos, A., & DeJong, J. (2006). Reducing child poverty with cash transfers: A sure thing? *Development Policy Review, 24*(5), 537–552.

Bernard, T., Dercon, S., Orkin, K., & Taffesse, A. (2014). *The future in mind: Aspirations and forward-looking behavior in rural Ethiopia* (Discussion Paper No. 10224). Oxford, UK: Center for Economic Research. Retrieved from http://www.cepr.org/active/publications/discussion_papers/dp.php?dpno=10224

Blank, R. M. (2006). What did the 1990s welfare reforms accomplish? In A. J. Auerbach, D. Card, & J. M. Quigley (Eds.), *Public policy and the income distribution* (pp. 33–79). New York: Russell Sage Foundation.

Blank, R. M. (2009). What we know, what we don't know, and what we need to know about welfare reform. In J. P. Ziliak (Ed.), *Welfare reform and its long-term consequences for America's poor* (pp. 22–58). Cambridge, UK: Cambridge University Press.

Boermel, A. (2011). Older people and the (un)caring state in "China's Manhattan." In B. Carrillo & J. Duckett (Eds.), *China's changing welfare mix: Local perspectives* (pp. 171–192). London: Routledge.

Brandt, L., & Holz, C. A. (2006). Spatial price differences in China: Estimates and implications. *Economic Development and Cultural Change, 55*(1), 43–86.

Brockmann, H., Delhey, J., Welzel, C., Yuan, H. (2009). The China puzzle: Falling happiness in a rising economy. *Journal of Happiness Studies, 10*(4), 387–405.

Brown, A. N., Cameron, D. B., & Wood, B. D. K. (2014). Quality evidence for policymaking: I'll believe it when I see the replication. *Journal of Development Effectiveness, 6*(3), 215–235.

Brown, P. (2002). *Poverty and leadership in the later Roman Empire.* London: University Press of New England.

Carrillo, B., & Duckett, J. (Eds.). (2011). *China's changing welfare mix: Local perspectives.* London: Routledge.

Case, A., & Deaton, A. (1998). Large cash transfers to the elderly in South Africa. *The Economic Journal, 108,* 1330–1361.

Chang, X., Chang, J., & Yuan, S. (2012). Nongcun Dibao jiating de fenxi yanjiu: Jiyu Shanghai de diaocha shuju [An analysis of rural Dibao families: Evidence from Shanghai]. *Dangdai Shijie Yu Shehui Zhuyi* [Contemporary World and Socialism], 5, 180–183.

Chen, H., Wong, Y., Zeng, Q., & Hämäläinen, J. (2013). Trapped in poverty? A study of the dibao programme in Shanghai. *China Journal of Social Work, 6*(3), 327–343.

Chen, J. Y. (2012). *Guilty of indigence: The urban poor in China, 1900–1953.* Princeton, NJ: Princeton University Press.

Chen, S., Ravallion, M., & Wang, Y. (2006). *Di bao: A guaranteed minimum income in China's cities?* (Working Paper No. 3805). Washington, DC: World Bank Policy Research. Retrieved from https://openknowledge.worldbank.org/bitstream/handle/10986/8831/wps3805.pdf?sequence=1

Cheung, C. K., & Leung, K. K. (2004). Forming life satisfaction among different social groups during the modernization of China. *Journal of Happiness Studies, 5,* 23–56.

Chiapa, C., Garrido, J., & Prina, S. (2012). The effect of social programs and exposure to professionals on the educational aspirations of the poor. *Economics of Education Review, 31,* 778–798.

Coady, D., Grosh, M. E., & Hoddinott, J. (2004). *Targeting of transfers in developing countries: Review of lessons and experience* (Vol. 1). Washington, DC: World Bank and International Food Policy Research Institute.

Cook, S. (2011). Global discourses, national policies, local outcomes: Reflections on China's welfare reforms. In B. Carrillo & J. Duckett (Eds.), *China's changing welfare mix: Local perspectives* (pp. 211–222). London: Routledge.

Cornia, J., & Stewart, F. (1993). Two errors of targeting. *Journal of International Development, 5*(5), 459–496.

Croll, E. J. (1999). Social welfare reform: Trends and tensions. *The China Quarterly, 159,* 684–699.

Dacheux, E., & Goujon, D. (2012). The solidarity economy: An alternative development strategy? *International Social Science Journal, 62*(203–204), 205–215.

Dahl, G. B., & Lochner, L. (2012). The impact of family income on child achievement: Evidence from the earned income tax credit. *The American Economic Review, 102*(5), 1927–1956.

Das, J., Do, Q., & Özler, B. (2005). Reassessing conditional cash transfer programs. *World Bank Research Observer, 20*(1), 57–80.

Dasso, R., & Fernandez, F. (2014). *Temptation goods and conditional cash transfers in Peru.* Working paper. Washington, DC. Retrieved from http://aswede. iies.su.se/papers/ASWEDE_C1_Fernandez.pdf

Davis, D. (1989). Chinese social welfare: Policies and outcomes. *The China Quarterly, 119,* 577–597.

Davis, D. (2005). Urban consumer culture. *The China Quarterly, 183,* 677–694.

de Brauw, A., & Rozelle, S. (2007). Returns to education in rural China. In E. C. Hannum & A. Park (Eds.), *Education and Reform in China* (pp. 207–223). London and New York: Routledge.

Dehejia, R. H., & Wahba, S. (2002). Propensity score-matching methods for nonexperimental causal studies. *The Review of Economics & Statistics, 84*(1), 151–161.

de Janvry, A., & Sadoulet, E. (2006). Making conditional cash transfer programs more efficient: Designing for maximum effect of the conditionality. *World Bank Economic Review, 20*(1), 1–29.

Deng, Q., & Li, S. (2010). *Nongcun dibao zhengce de fupin xiaoguo pinggu* [Assessment of the rural Minimum Living Standard Guarantee programme's effects]. Background paper prepared for the Evaluation Report of the Effect of China's Rural Poverty Alleviation and Development Outline (2001–2010). Beijing.

Devereux, S., Marshall, J., MacAskill, J., & Pelham, L. (2005). Making cash count: Lessons from cash transfer schemes in East and Southern Africa for supporting the most vulnerable children and households (Policy Report). New York: United Nations Children's Fund. London and Brighton: Save the Children, HelpAge International, and Institute of Development Studies.

Diaz, J. J., & Handa, S. (2006). An assessment of propensity score matching as nonexperimental impact estimator: Evidence from Mexico's PROGRESA program. *Journal of Human Resources*, 41(2), 319–345.

Dixon, J. E. (1981). *The Chinese welfare system 1949–1979*. New York: Praeger Publishers.

Dizon-Ross, R. (2014). *Parents' perceptions and children's education: Experimental evidence from Malawi*. Unpublished manuscript. Cambridge, MA: Massachusetts Institute of Technology. Retrieved from http://studentsocial-support.org/files/s3rd/files/dizon-ross.pdf

Dover, M. A., & Joseph, B. H. R. (2008). Human needs: Overview. In T. Mizrahi & L. E. Davis (Eds.), *Encyclopedia of social work* (20th ed.) (pp. 398–406). Washington, DC: National Association of Social Workers & New York: Oxford University Press.

Du, Y., & Park, A. (2007). Zhongguo de chengshi pingkun: Shehui jiuzhu ji qi xiaoying [Social assistance programs and their effects on poverty reduction in urban China]. *Jingji Yanjiu* [Economic Research], 12, 24–33.

Duan, S. (2015, April 14). Kaizhan shinei fupin, Dongguan 1/3 dibaohu shixian tuopin [Dongguan launched city anti-poverty campaign, 1/3 Dibao recipients escaped poverty]. *Nanfang Ribao* [Nanfang Daily]. Retrieved from http://dg.southcn.com/content/2015-04/14/content_122132582.htm

Duckett, J. (2011). *The Chinese state's retreat from health: Policy and the politics of retrenchment*. London: Routledge.

Duckett, J. (2012). China's 21st-century welfare reforms. *Local Economy*, 27(5–6), 645–650.

Duflo, E. (2003). Grandmothers and granddaughters: Old age pension and intrahousehold allocation in South Africa. *World Bank Economic Review*, 17(1), 1–25.

Eardley, T., Bradshaw, J., Ditch, J., Gough, I., & Whiteford, P. (1996). *Social assistance in OECD countries* (Vol. I): *Synthesis Report* (Research Report No. 46). UK Department of Social Security. London: HMSO. Retrieved from http://www.canadiansocialresearch.net/rrep046.pdf

Easterlin, R. (2001). Income and happiness: Towards a unified theory. *The Economic Journal*, 111(July), 465–484.

Edin, K. J., & Shaefer, H. L. (2015). *$2.00 a Day: Living on almost nothing in America*. Boston & New York: Houghton Mifflin Harcourt.

Ellwood, D. T. (1988). *Poor support: Poverty in the American family*. New York: Basic Books.

Evans, D. K., & Popova, A. (2014). *Cash transfers and temptation goods: A review of global evidence* (Working Paper No. 6886). Washington, DC: World

Bank Group. Retrieved from http://documents.worldbank.org/curated/en/617631468001808739/pdf/WPS6886.pdf

Evans, W. N., & Garthwaite, C. L. (2014). Giving mom a break: The impact of higher EITC payments on maternal health. *American Economic Journal: Economic Policy, 6*(2), 258–290.

Feng, S., Hu, Y., & Moffitt, R. A. (2015). *Long run trends in unemployment and labor force participation in China* (NBER Working Paper No. 21460). Retrieved from http://www.nber.org/papers/w21460

Fiszbein, A., Schady, N., Ferreira, F. H. G., Grosh, M., Kelleher, N., Olinto, P., & Skoufias, E. (2009). *Conditional cash transfers: Reducing present and future poverty*. Washington, DC: World Bank. Retrieved from https://openknowledge.worldbank.org/handle/10986/2597

Foster, J., Greer, J., & Thorbecke, E. (1984). A class of decomposable poverty measures. *Econometrica: Journal of the Econometric Society*, 761–766.

Frazier, M. W. (2014) State schemes or safety nets? China's push for universal coverage. *Daedalus, 143*(2), 69–80.

Frey, B., & Stutzer, A. (2002). *Happiness and economics: How the economy and institutions affect human well-being*. Princeton, NJ: Princeton University Press.

Gao, Q. (2006). The social benefit system in urban China: Reforms and trends from 1988 to 2002. *Journal of East Asian Studies, 6*(1), 31–67.

Gao, Q. (2013). Public assistance and poverty reduction: The case of Shanghai. *Global Social Policy, 13*(2), 193–215.

Gao, Q. (2015). From welfare to work: Effectiveness of a job training program in Shanghai. Working paper.

Gao, G., Chen, D., & Cui, H. (2013). Zichan jilie yu Dibao jiuzhu zhidu: Jiyu chengshi Dibao jiating zichan zhuangkuang de diaocha yu bijiao yanjiu [Asset cumulation and minimum livelihood ganrantee: A survey and comparative study of assets among urban Dibao families]. *Nantong Daxue Xuebao* [Journal of Nantong University Social Science Edition], *29*(2), 51–63.

Gao, Q., Garfinkel, I., & Zhai, F. (2009). Anti-poverty effectiveness of the minimum living standard assistance policy in urban China. *Review of Income & Wealth, 55*(s1), 630–655.

Gao, Q., Kaushal, N., & Waldfogel, J. (2009). How have expansions in the Earned Income Tax Credit affected family expenditures? In J. Ziliak. (Ed.), *Ten years after: Evaluating the long-term effects of welfare reform on children, families, welfare, and work* (pp. 104–139). New York: Cambridge University Press.

Gao, Q., & Riskin, C. (2009). Market versus social benefits: Explaining China's changing income inequality. In D. Davis & F. Wang (Eds.), *Creating wealth and poverty in postsocialist China* (pp. 20–36). Palo Alto, CA: Stanford University Press.

Gao, Q., & Riskin, C. (2013). Generosity and participation: Variations in urban China's Minimum Livelihood Guarantee policy. In D. Kennedy & J. E. Stiglitz.

(Eds.), *Law & economics with Chinese characteristics: Institutions for promoting development in the 21st century* (pp. 393–422). Oxford, UK: Oxford University Press.

Gao, Q., & Wang, X. (2016). Does welfare receipt discourage social participation? Evidence from China. Working paper.

Gao, Q., Wu, S., Wu, Q., & Zhai, F. (2016). Welfare participation and subjective well-being in China: The role of perceived social Class. Working paper.

Gao, Q., Wu, S., & Zhai, F. (2015). Welfare participation and time use in China. *Social Indicators Research, 124,* 863–887.

Gao, Q., Yang, S., & Li, S. (2013). The Chinese welfare state in transition: 1988-2007. *Journal of Social Policy, 42*(4), 743–762.

Gao, Q., Yang, S., & Li, S. (2015). Welfare, targeting, and anti-poverty effectiveness: The case of urban China. *Quarterly Review of Economics and Finance, 56,* 30–42.

Gao, Q., Yoo, J. Y., Yang, S., & Zhai, F. (2011). Welfare residualism: A comparative study of the basic livelihood security systems in China & South Korea. *International Journal of Social Welfare, 20,* 113–124.

Gao, Q., & Zhai, F. (2012). Anti-poverty family policies in China: A critical evaluation. *Asian Social Work and Policy Review, 6*(1), 122–135.

Gao, Q., & Zhai, F. (2015). Public assistance, economic prospect, and happiness in urban China. *Social Indicators Research.* doi:10.1007/s11205-015-1174-4.

Gao, Q., Zhai, F., & Garfinkel, I. (2010). How does public assistance affect family expenditures? The case of urban China. *World Development, 38*(7), 989–1000.

Gao, Q., Zhai, F., Yang, S. & Li, S. (2014). Does welfare enable family expenditures on human capital? Evidence from China. *World Development, 64,* 219–231.

Garfinkel, I., Rainwater, L., & Smeeding, T. (2010). *Wealth and welfare states: Is America a laggard or leader?* New York: Oxford University Press.

Gentilini, U., Maddalena, H., & Ruslan, Y. (2014). *The state of social safety nets 2014.* Washington, DC: World Bank Group.

Golan, J., Sicular, T., & Umapathi, N. (2014). *Any guarantees? China's rural minimum living standard guarantee program* (Social Protection and Labor Discussion Paper No. 1423). Washington, DC: World Bank Group. Retrieved from http://documents.worldbank.org/curated/en/464451468154454071/pdf/900300NWP0P132085299B00PUBLIC001423.pdf

Golley, J., & Kong, S. T. (2013). Inequality in the intergenerational mobility of education in China. *China and World Economy, 21*(2), 15–37.

Grosh, M., del Ninno, C., Tesliuc, E., & Ouerghi, A. (2008). *For protection and promotion: the design and implementation of effective safety nets.* Washington, DC: The World Bank. Retrieved from http://siteresources.worldbank.org/SPLP/Resources/461653-1207162275268/For_Protection_and_Promotion908.pdf

Guan, X. (2005). *Zhongguo chengshi pingkun wenti gaisu* [Poverty in urban China: An introduction]. Retrieved from http://www.chinasocialpolicy.org/Paper_Show.asp?Paper_ID=40.

Guan, X., & Xu, B. (2011). Central-local relations in social policy and the development of urban and rural social assistance programmes. In B. Carrillo & J. Duckett (Eds.), *China's changing welfare mix: Local perspectives* (pp. 20–35). London: Routledge.

Gustafsson, B., & Deng, Q. (2011). Di Bao receipt and its importance for combating poverty in urban China. *Poverty & Public Policy, 3*(1), 1–32.

Gustafsson, B., & Gang, S. (2013). A comparison of social assistance in China and Sweden. *China Journal of Social Work, 6*(3), 292–310.

Gustafsson, B., Sicular, T., & Li, S. (2008). *Income inequality and public policy in China*. Cambridge, UK: Cambridge University Press.

Hammond, D. (2011). Local variation in urban social assistance: Community public service agencies in Dalian. In B. Carrillo & J. Duckett (Eds.), *China's changing welfare mix: Local perspectives* (pp. 64–81). London: Routledge.

Han, H., Gao, Q., & Xu, Y. (2016). Welfare participation and family consumption choices in rural China. *Global Social Welfare, 3*(4), 223–241.

Han, H., & Xu, Y. (2013). Nongcun zuidi shenghuo baozhang zhidu de biaozhun xiaoguo yanjiu [A study on the poverty targeting of the minimum living standard security (MLSS) scheme in rural China: Evidence from Henan and Shanxi provinces]. *Zhongguo Renkou Kexue* [Chinese Journal of Population Science], *4*, 117–125.

Han, H., & Xu, Y. (2014). Zhongguo nongcun Dibao zhidu de fanpinkun yanjiu xiaoying [The anti-poverty effectiveness of the minimum living standard assistance policy in rural China: Evidence from five central and western provinces]. *Jingji Pinglun* [Economic Review], *6*, 63–77.

Han, K. (Ed.). (2012). *Chengshi Dibao fangtanlu* [Interviews with Minimum Livelihood Guarantee recipients in urban China]. Jinan, China: Shandong Renmin Press.

Han, K., & Guo, Y. (2012). Fuli yilai shi fou cunzai? [Does welfare dependency exist?]. *Shehuixue Yanjiu* [Sociological Research], *2*, 149–67.

Handa, S., & Maluccio, J. A. (2008). Matching the gold standard: Comparing experimental and non-experimental evaluation techniques for a geographically targeted program (Discussion Paper No. 08-13). Middlebury, VT: Middlebury College Economics. Retrieved from http://www.unc.edu/~shanda/research/matching_handa_maluccio_sept08.pdf

Hands, A. (1968). *Charities and social aid in Greece and Rome*. Ithaca, NY: Cornell University Press.

Hannum, E. C., & Adams, J. H. (2008). Beyond cost: Rural perspectives on barriers to education. In D. Davis & F. Wang (Eds.), *Creating wealth and poverty in China* (pp. 156–171). Palo Alto, CA: Stanford University Press.

Hannum, E. C., Wang, M., & Adams, J. H. (2008). Urban-rural disparities in access to primary and secondary education under market reform. In M. K. Whyte (Ed.), *One country, two societies? Rural-urban inequality in contemporary China* (pp. 125–146). Cambridge, MA: Harvard University Press.

Harvey, A. S. (2004). Welcome address of the IATUR president: eIJTUR and time use: Past, present and future. *Electronic International Journal of Time Use Research. 1*(1), I–V.

Haushofer, J., & Shapiro, J. (2016). The short-term impact of unconditional cash transfers to the poor: Evidence from Kenya. *Quarterly Journal of Economics.* doi:10.1093/qje/qjw025.

Hoddinott, J., & Skoufias, E. (2004). The impact of PROGRESA on food consumption. *Economic Development and Cultural Change, 53*(1), 37–61.

Hong, D. (2005a). *Chengshi jumin zuidi shenghuo baozhang biaozhun* [The Minimum Livelihood Guarantee standards for urban residents]. Retrieved from http://www.chinasocialpolicy.org/Paper_Show.asp?Paper_ID=40.

Hong, D. (2005b). *Chengshi jumin zuidi shenghuo baozhang zhidu de zuixin fazhan.* [Recent developments in the Minimum Livelihood Guarantee policy for urban residents]. Retrieved from http://www.chinasocialpolicy.org/Paper_Show.asp?Paper_ID=38.

Hotz, V. J., & Scholz, J. K. (2003). The Earned Income Tax Credit. In R. A. Moffitt (Ed.), *Means-tested transfer programs in the United States* (pp. 141–198). Chicago, IL: University of Chicago Press.

Hoynes, H. (2014). A revolution in poverty policy: The Earned Income Tax Credit and the well-being of American families. *Pathways: A Magazine on Poverty, Inequality, and Social Policy, Summer,* 23–27. Retrieved from http://web.stanford.edu/group/scspi/_media/pdf/pathways/summer_2014/Pathways_Summer_2014.pdf

Hu, X., Gao, L., & Cui, H. (2013). Chenshi Dibao jiating shengcun zhuangkuang shizheng fenxi [An empirical analysis of the living conditions of urban Dibao families]. *Jinan daxue xuebao (shehui kexue ban)* [Journal of Jinan University Social Science Edition], *23*(2), 58–63.

Huang, J., Wu, S., & Deng, S. (2015). Relative income, relative assets, and happiness in urban China. *Social Indicators Research.* doi:10.1007/s11205-015-0936-3.

Huang, X. (2015). Four worlds of welfare in China: Understanding subnational variation in Chinese social health insurance. *The China Quarterly, 222,* 449–474.

Huang, X., & Gao, Q. (2015). Do the "carrots" work? Effect of social welfare on regime support in China. Working paper.

Hussain, A. (2007). Social security in transition. In V. Shue & C. Wong (Eds.), *Paying for progress in China: Public finance, human welfare and changing patterns of inequality* (pp. 96–116). New York: Routledge.

Jalan, J., & Ravallion, M. (2003). Estimating the benefit incidence of an antipoverty program by propensity-score matching. *Journal of Business & Economic Statistics, 21*(1), 19–30.

Jensen, R. (2010). The (perceived) returns to education and the demand for schooling. *The Quarterly Journal of Economics, 125*(2), 515–548.

Kaushal, N., & Gao, Q. (2011). Food Stamp program and consumption choices in low-educated single mother families. In M. Grossman (Ed.), *Economic aspects of obesity* (pp. 223–248). Chicago, IL: University of Chicago Press.

Kaushal, N., Gao, Q., & Waldfogel, J. (2007). Welfare reform and family expenditures: How are single mothers adapting to the new welfare and work regime? *Social Service Review, 81*(3), 369–398.

Khan, A. R. (2004). *Growth, inequality and poverty in China: A comparative study of the experience in the periods before and after the Asian crisis* (Discussion Paper No. 15). Employment and Poverty. Geneva, Switzerland: International Labour Office (ILO).

Khan, A. R., & Riskin, C. (2001). *Inequality and poverty in China in the age of globalization.* New York: Oxford University Press.

Khan, A. R., & Riskin, C. (2005). China's household income and its distribution, 1995 and 2002. *The China Quarterly, 182,* 356–384.

Kim, Y., Zou, L., Joo, Y. S., & Sherraden, M. (2011). *Asset-based policy in South Korea* (CSD Publication No. 11-22). St. Louis, MO: George Warren Brown School of Social Work Center for Social Development. Retrieved from http://csd.wustl.edu/Publications/Documents/PB11-22.pdf

Kirp, D. L. (2015, August 8). What do the poor need? Try asking them. *The New York Times Sunday Review.* Retrieved from http://www.nytimes.com/2015/08/09/opinion/sunday/david-l-kirp-what-do-the-poor-need-try-asking-them.html

Kitsios, G. D., Dahabreh, I. J., Callahan, S., Paulus, J. K., Campagna, A. C., & Dargin, J. M. (2015). Can we trust observational studies using propensity scores in the critical care literature? A systematic comparison with randomized clinical trials. *Critical Care Medicine, 43*(9), 1870–1879.

Knight, J., & Gunatilaka, R. (2011). Does economic growth raise happiness in China? *Oxford Development Studies, 39*(1), 1–24.

Lan, J. (2015, January 14). Dibao shenqing xiang dabing jiating jiangdi menkan, shouti "jiuzhu jiantui" [Dibao lowers application criteria for families with seriously ill members and launches "gradual income disregard"]. *Beijing Wanbao* [Beijing Evening News]. Retrieved from http://www.chinanews.com/gn/2015/01-14/6968968.shtml

Layard, R. (2005). *Happiness: Lessens from a new science.* London and New York: Penguin Books.

Lee, J., & Zhou, M. (2004). *Asian American youth: Culture, identity, and ethnicity.* New York: Routledge.

Lee, J., & Zhou, M. (2015). *The Asian American achievement paradox.* New York: Russell Sage.

Lei, X., & Lin, W. (2009). The new cooperative medical scheme in rural China: Does more coverage mean more service and better health? *Health Economics, 18*(2), 25–46.

Leung, J. C. (2003). Social security reforms in China: Issues and prospects. *International Journal of Social Welfare, 12*(2), 73–85.

Leung, J. C. (2006). The emergence of social assistance in China. *International Journal of Social Welfare, 15*(3), 188–198.

Leung, J. C., & Nann, R. C. (1995). *Authority and benevolence: Social welfare in China.* Hong Kong: The Chinese University Press.

Leung, J. C., & Xu, Y. (2015). *China's social welfare: The third turning point.* Cambridge, UK: Polity Press.

Li, S., Sato, H., & Sicular, T. (2013). *Rising inequality in China: Challenge to a harmonious Society.* Cambridge, UK: Cambridge University Press.

Li, S., & Sicular, T. (2014). The distribution of household income in China: Inequality, poverty, and policies. *China Quarterly, 217,* 1–41.

Li, S., & Yang, S. (2009). Zhongguo chengzhen dibao zhengce dui shouru fenpei he pinkun de yingxiang zuoyong [Impacts of China's urban dibao policy on income distribution and poverty]. *Zhongguo renkou kexue* [Chinese Journal of Population Science], *5,* 11–20.

Liang, X., Guo, H., Jin, C., Peng, X., & Zhang, X. (2012). The effect of new cooperative medical scheme on health outcomes and alleviating catastrophic health expenditure in China: A systematic review. *Plos One, 7*(8), 1–11.

Liu, D., & Tsegao, D. (2011). The new cooperative medical scheme (NCMS) and its implications for access to health care and medical expenditure: Evidence from rural China (Discussion Paper on Development Policy No. 155). Bonn, Germany: The Center for Development Research. Retrieved from http://age-consearch.umn.edu/bitstream/116746/2/DP155.pdf

Liu, J. (2011). Life goes on: Redundant women workers in Nanjing. In B. Carrillo & J. Duckett (Eds.), *China's changing welfare mix: Local perspectives* (pp. 82–103). London: Routledge.

Liu, K., Wu, Q., & Liu, J. (2014). Examining the association between social health insurance participation and patients' out-of-pocket payments in China: The role of institutional arrangement. *Social Science & Medicine, 113,* 95–103.

Liu, X. (2010). Jianguo 60 nian lai woguo shehui jiuzhu fazhan lichen yu zhidu bianqian [Development process and institutional change of China's social assistance: 1949-2009]. *Huazhong shifan daxue xuebao (renwen shehui kexue ban)* [Journal of Huazhong Normal University (Humanities and Social Sciences)], *49*(4), 19–26.

Long, Q., Xu, L., Bekedam, H., & Tang, S. (2013). Changes in health expenditures in China in 2000s: Has the health system reform improved affordability? *International Journal for Equity in Health, 12*(40), 1–8.

Long, Q., Zhang, T., Xu, L., Tang, S., & Hemminki, E. (2010). Utilisation of maternal health care in western rural China under a new rural health insurance system (New Co-operative Medical System). *Tropical Medicine & International Health, 15* (10), 1210–1217.

Lora-Wainwright, A. (2011). "If you can walk and eat, you don't go to hospital": The quest for healthcare in rural Sichuan. In B. Carrillo & J. Duckett (Eds.), *China's changing welfare mix: Local perspectives* (pp. 104–125). London: Routledge.

Lu, S., Lin, Y. T., Vikse, J. H., & Huang, C. C. (2013). Effectiveness of social welfare programmes on poverty reduction and income inequality in China. *Journal of Asian Public Policy, 6*(3), 277–291.

Mani, A., Mullainathan, S., Shafir, E., & Zhao, J. (2013). Poverty impedes cognitive function. *Science, 341*, 976–980.

Maxfield, M. (2013). *The effects of the Earned Income Tax Credit on child achievement and long-term educational attainment.* Michigan State University. Retrieved from https://www.msu.edu/~maxfiel7/20131114%20Maxfield%20 EITC%20Child%20Education.pdf

Meyer, B. (2010). The effects of the Earned Income Tax Credit and recent reforms. In J. R. Brown (Ed.), *National Bureau of Economic Research book series tax policy and the economy, Volume 24* (pp. 153–180). Chicago, IL: University of Chicago Press.

Meyer, B., & Sullivan, J. X. (2008). Changes in the consumption, income, and well-being of single mother headed families. *American Economic Review, 98*(5), 2221–2241.

Milligan, K., & Stabile, M. (2011). Do child tax benefits affect the well-being of children? Evidence from Canadian child benefit expansions. *American Economic Journal: Economic Policy, 3*(3), 175–205.

Ministry of Civil Affairs [MCA]. (2015a). *Dibao jidu baobiao* [Quarterly statistics on Dibao]. Beijing: Ministry of Civil Affairs. Retrieved from http://www. mca.gov.cn/article/sj/tjjb/dbsj/.

Ministry of Civil Affairs [MCA]. (2015b). *Shehui fuwu tongji jibao (2014 nian 4 jidu)* [Quarterly Statistical Report on Social Services (fourth quarter of 2014)]. Beijing: Ministry of Civil Affairs. Retrieved from http://files2.mca.gov. cn/cws/201501/20150129172531166.htm

Ministry of Civil Affairs [MCA]. (1996–2014). *Zhongguo minzheng tongji nianjian* [China civil affairs' statistical yearbook]. Beijing: China Statistics Press.

Ministry of Health. (2009). *Zhongguo weisheng fuwu diaocha baogao, 2008 [An analysis report of national health services survey in China, 2008].* Beijing: Peking Union Medical College Press.

Ministry of Human Resources and Social Security [MHRSS]. (2010, March 30). Guanyu yinfa jinyibu zhenghe ziyuan, jiaqiang jiceng laodong jiuye shehui baozhang gonggong fuwu pingtai he wangluo jianshe zhidao yijian de tongzhi [Notification about further integrating resources, strengthening work support, and establishing public service platforms and networks]. Retrieved from http://www.mohrss.gov.cn/zcyjs/ZCYJSzhengcewenjian/201003/t20100330_ 83264.htm

Moffitt, R. A. (2003a). The Temporary Assistance to Needy Families Program. In R. A. Moffitt (Ed.), *Means-tested transfer programs in the United States* (pp. 293–364). Chicago and London: University of Chicago Press.

Moffitt, R. A. (Ed.). (2003b). *Means-tested transfer programs in the United States.* Chicago and London: University of Chicago Press.

Moffitt, R. A. (2016). Economics of means-tested transfer programs: Introduction. In R. A. Moffitt (Ed.), *Means-tested programs in the United States: Volume I,* (pp. 1–20). Chicago and London: University of Chicago Press.

Mok, K. H., & Wong, Y. C. (2011). Regional disparities and education inequalities: City responses and coping strategies. In B. Carrillo & J. Duckett (Eds.), *China's changing welfare mix: Local perspectives* (pp. 126–156). London: Routledge.

Mullainathan, S. & Shafir, E. (2013). *Scarcity: Why having too little means so much.* New York: Times Books.

National Bureau of Statistics [NBS]. (2005–2010a). *Zhongguo laodong tongji nianjian* [China labor statistical yearbook]. Beijing, China: China Statistics Press.

National Bureau of Statistics [NBS]. (1996–2014b). *Zhongguo tongji nianjian* [China statistical yearbooks]. Beijing, China: Statistical Press.

Nichols, A., & Rothstein, J. (2016). The Earned Income Tax Credit. In R. A. Moffitt (Ed.), *Means-tested programs in the United States: Volume I* (pp. 137–218). Chicago and London: University of Chicago Press.

Nguyen, T. (2013). Information, role models and perceived returns to education: Experimental evidence from Madagascar. enGender Impact: World Bank's Gender Impact Evaluation Database. Washington, DC: World Bank. Retrieved from http://documents.worldbank.org/curated/en/2013/08/18310765/information-role-models-perceived-returns-education-experimental-evidence-madagascar

O'Keefe, P. (2004). *Social assistance in China: An evolving system.* mimeo. World Bank, Washington, DC.

Ranganathan, M., & Lagarde, M. (2012). Promoting healthy behaviours and improving health outcomes in low and middle income countries: A review of the impact of conditional cash transfer programmes. *Preventive Medicine, 55,* 95–105.

Ravallion, M. (2009). How relevant is targeting to the success of an antipoverty program? *The World Bank Research Observer, 24*(2), 205–231.

Ravallion, M., & Chen, S. (2015). Benefit incidence with incentive effects, measurement errors and latent heterogeneity: A case study for China. *Journal of Public Economics, 128,* 124–132.

Rawlings, L. B., & Rubio, G. M. (2005). Evaluating the impact of conditional cash transfer programs. *The World Bank Research Observer, 20*(1), 29–55.

Ren, Y., Zeng, L., & Yang, X. (2015). Chengxiang yiliao jiuzhu zhidu zhi xianzhuang, wenti yu duice [The status quo, problems and solutions of the urban and rural medical assistance system]. *Nanjing Yike Daxue Xuebao*

(Shehui Kexue) [Acta Universitatis Medicinalis Nanjing (Social Sciences)], *1*, 11–14.

Riskin, C., Zhao, R., & Li, S. (2001). *China's retreat from equality: Income distribution & economic transition.* Armonk, NY: M. E. Sharpe, Inc.

Robertson, L., Mushati, P., Eaton, J., Dumba, L., Mavise, G., Makoni, J., Schumacher, C., Crea, T., Monasch, R., Sherr, L., Garnett, G., Nyamukapa, C., & Gregson, S. (2013). Effects of unconditional and conditional cash transfers on child health and development in Zimbabwe: A cluster-randomised trial. *Lancet, 381*, 1283–1292.

Rosenbaum, P. R., & Rubin, D. B. (1983). The central role of the propensity score in observational studies for causal effects. *Biometrika, 70*(1), 41–55.

Saich, A. (2008). *Providing public goods in transitional China.* London and New York: Palgrave Macmillan.

Saich, A. (2015). *The governance and politics of China.* London and New York: Palgrave Macmillan.

Saunders, P., & Shang, X. (2001). Social security reform in China's transition to a market economy. *Social Policy & Administration, 35*(3), 274–289.

Shanghai Bureau of Civil Affairs. (2003, March 31). *Guanyu shidang tiaozheng Dibao jiating chengyuan jiuye hou "jiuzhu jiantui" zhaogu shijian youguan shixiang de tongzhi* [Notification about adjusting the schedule for gradual reduction of benefits among Dibao recipients who obtain jobs, issued jointly]. Retrieved from http://www.shmzj.gov.cn/gb/shmzj/node8/node15/node55/node229/node277/userobject1ai7991.html

Shanghai Bureau of Civil Affairs. (2015, April, 3). *Guanyu tiaozheng tigao benshi chenxiang Dibao jiating jiuye renyuan shouru huomian biaozhun de tongzhi* [Notification about raising the income disregard level for Dibao recipients who obtain jobs]. Retrieved from http://www.shmzj.gov.cn/gb/shmzj/node8/node15/node55/node229/node277/u1ai39653.html

Shi, W., Chongsuvivatwong, V., Geater, A., Zhang, J., Zhang, H., & Brombal, D. (2010). The influence of the rural health security schemes on health utilization and household impoverishment in rural China: Data from a household survey of western and central China. *International Journal for Equity in Health, 9*(7), 1–11.

Slaughter, A. (2015). *Unfinished business: Women, men, work, family.* New York: Random House.

Smyth, R., Nielsen, I., & Zhai, Q. (2010). Personal well-being in urban China. *Social Indicators Research, 95*, 231–251.

Soares, F. V., Ribas, R. P., & Osório, R. G. (2010). Evaluating the impact of Brazil's Bolsa familia: Cash transfer programs in comparative perspective. *Latin American Research Review, 45*(2), 173–190.

Solinger, D. J. (2009). The phase-out of the unfit: Keeping the unworthy out of work. In L. A. Keister (Ed.), *Research in the sociology of work* (Vol. 19): *Work and organizations in China after thirty years of transition* (pp. 307–336). London: Emerald Press.

Solinger, D. J. (2010). The urban Dibao: Guarantee for minimum livelihood or for minimal turmoil? In F. Wu & C. J. Webster (Eds.), *Marginalization in China: Comparative perspectives* (pp. 253–277). New York: Palgrave Macmillan.

Solinger, D. J. (2011). Dibaohu in distress: The meager Minimum Livelihood Guarantee system in Wuhan. In B. Carillo & J. Duckett (Eds.), *China's changing welfare mix: Local perspectives* (pp. 36–63). London: Routledge.

Solinger, D. J. (2012). The new urban underclass and its consciousness: Is it a class? *Journal of Contemporary China, 21*(78), 1011–1028.

Solinger, D. J. (2013). Streets as suspect: State skepticism and the current losers in urban China. *Critical Asian Studies, 45*(1), 3–26.

Solinger, D. J. (2015a). *Report on the employment conditions of unemployed workers*. Working paper submitted to the Ford Foundation Global Travel and Learning Fund.

Solinger, D. J. (2015b, August). *Justice and the poor: The Minimum Livelihood Guarantee in the period of Xi Jinping*. Paper presented at the conference Accountability and Control in the Xi Jinping Era. Melbourne, Australia: University of Melbourne.

Solinger, D. J., & Hu, Y. (2012). Welfare, wealth, and poverty in urban China: The Dibao and its differential disbursement. *China Quarterly, 211*, 741–764.

Solinger, D. J., & Jiang, T. (2016). When Chinese central orders and promotion criteria conflict: Implementation decisions on the destitute in poor versus prosperous cities. *Modern China, 42*(6), 571–606.

State Council Information Office [SCIO]. (2004). *Zhong guo de she hui bao zhang zhuang kuang he zheng ce bai pi shu* [White paper on China's social security and its policy]. Beijing, China: State Council Information Office of the People's Republic of China.

State Council Information Office [SCIO]. (2014). *Zhongguo de shehui baozhang Zhuangkuang he zhengce baipishu* [White paper on China's social security and its policy]. Beijing, China: State Council Information Office of the People's Republic of China.

Sun, Q., Liu, X., Meng, Q., Tang, S., Yu, B., & Tolhurst, R. (2009). Evaluating the financial protection of patients with chronic disease by health insurance in rural China. *International Journal for Equity in Health, 8*(28), 3567–3579.

Sun, X., Jackson, S., Carmichael, G., & Sleigh, A. (2009). Catastrophic medical payment and financial protection in rural China: Evidence from the new cooperative medical scheme in Shandong province. *Health Economics, 18*(1), 103–119.

Tang, J. (2004). Zhongguo chengxiang Dibao zhidu de xianzhuang yu qianzhan [The situation and prospects of the Minimum Livelihood Guarantee program]. In X. Ru, X. Lu, & P. Li (Eds.), *Zhongguo shehui xingshi fenxi yu yuce* [Analysis and prediction of China's social situation]. Beijing: Social Sciences Documentation Press.

Tang, J., Sha, L., & Ren, Z. (2003). *Zhongguo chengshi pinkun yu fanpinkun baogao* [Report on poverty and anti-poverty initiatives in urban China]. Beijing: Huaxia Press.

Umapathi, N., Wang, D., & O'Keefe, P. (2013). *Eligibility thresholds for Minimum Living Guarantee programs: International practices and implications for China* (Discussion Paper Series No. 1307). Washington, DC: World Bank Social Protection & Labor. Retrieved from https://openknowledge.worldbank.org/handle/10986/17006

Wagstaff, A., Lindelow, M., Gao, J., Xu, L., & Qian, J. (2009). Extending health insurance to the rural population: An impact evaluation of China's new cooperative medical scheme. *Journal of Health Economics, 28*(1), 1–19.

Wang, H., Cheng, Z., & Smyth, R. (2015). *Does consuming more make you happier? Evidence from Chinese panel data* (Discussion Paper No. 21). Helsinki, Finland: The Bank of Finland Institute for Economies in Transition (BOFIT). Retrieved from http://www.suomenpankki.fi/bofit_en/tutkimus/tutkimusjulkaisut/dp/Documents/2015/dp2115.pdf

Wang, K. (2009). *Chenshi Dibao jiating jiaoyu jiuzhu wenti yanjiu* [Education assistance among urban Dibao families: Evidence from Yuwangtai district, Kaifeng, Henan] (Master's thesis). Henan University, Henan, China.

Wang, M. (2007). Emerging urban poverty and effects of the Dibao program on alleviating poverty in China. *China & World Economy, 15*(2), 74–88.

Wang, Q., Liu, J., Lu, Z., Luo, Q., & Liu, J. (2014). Role of the new rural cooperative medical system in alleviating catastrophic medical payments for hypertension, stroke and coronary heart disease in poor rural areas of China. *BMC Public Health, 14*, 1–10.

Wang, X. (2013, September 23). Measuring the width of the wealth gap. *Caixin Online*. Retrieved from http://english.caixin.com/2013-09-23/100585181.html?p2. Chinese version retrieved from http://topics.caixin.com/income-gap/

Wang, Y. (2006). Dui chengshi junmin zuidi shenghuo baozhang zhengce zhixing qingkuang de pingjia [The evaluation of the implementation of urban Dibao]. *Tongji Yanjiu* [Statistical Research], *10*, 49–54.

Wong, C. (2012). *Performance, monitoring, and evaluation in China* (Special Series on the Nuts & Bolts of M&E Systems No. 23). World Bank. Retrieved from https://openknowledge.worldbank.org/handle/10986/17083

Wong, G. K., & Yu, L. (2002). Income and social inequality in China: Impact on consumption and shopping patterns. *International Journal of Social Economics, 29*(5), 370–384.

Wong, L. (1998). *Marginalization and social welfare in China*. London: Routledge.

World Bank. (2011). *Reducing inequality for shared growth in China: Strategy and policy options for Guangdong province.* Washington, DC: The World Bank. https://openknowledge.worldbank.org/handle/10986/2251

World Bank. (2015). *The state of social safety nets 2015.* Washington, DC: World Bank Group. Retrieved from http://documents.worldbank.org/curated/en/2015/07/24741765/state-social-safety-nets-2015

Wu, A. M., & Ramesh, M. (2014). Poverty reduction in urban China: The impact of cash transfers. *Social Policy and Society, 13*(02), 285–299.

Xu, Y. (2013). *Building equitable opportunities into social assistance* (Project No. 44026-012). Asian Development Bank Report.

Yang, T., & Ge, D. (2002). Zhongguo chengshi shequ de shehui baozhang xin fanshi: Dalian yu Hangzhou shequ gean yanjiu yu tansuo. [A new paradigm of social security in urban China: a case study of Dalian and Huangzhou communities], *Management World,* (2), 57–64.

Yao, X., & Zhang, H. (2004). An analysis of the differential of the rates of return to schooling between urban and rural labor in China: Evidence from the survey in Zhejiang, Guangdong, Hunan and Anhui. *Collected Essays on Finance and Economics, 6,* 1–7.

Yip, W., & Hsiao, W. (2009). Non-evidence-based policy: How effective is China's new cooperative medical scheme in reducing medical impoverishment? *Social Science & Medicine, 68* (2), 201–209.

Zahoor, H., Luketich, J. D., Levy, R. M., Awais, O., Winger, D. G., Gibson, M. K., & Nason, K. S. (2015). A propensity-matched analysis comparing survival after primary minimally invasive esophagectomy followed by adjuvant therapy to neoadjuvant therapy for esophagogastric adenocarcinoma. *Journal of Thoracic and Cardiovascular Surgery, 149*(2), 538–547.

Zhang, X. (2012). Empirical analysis of difference of returns to education between rural and urban areas: Based on the data of CHIP 2002. *Journal of Xiamen University (Arts & Social Sciences), 6,* 118–125.

Zhang, X., & Xu, Y. (2006). *Zhongguo nongcun zuidi shenghuo baozhang zhidu yanjiu* [Research report on the rural Minimum Livelihood Guarantee system in China]. Asian Development Bank. Retrieved from http://www.adb.org/sites/default/files/project-document/73009/36656-01-prc-tacr-03.pdf

Ziliak, J. (Ed.). (2009). *Ten years after: Evaluating the long-term effects of welfare reform on children, families, welfare, and work.* New York: Cambridge University Press.

Ziliak, J. (2016). Temporary assistance for needy families. In R. Moffitt (Ed.), *Economics of means-tested transfer programs in the United States, Volume I* (pp. 303–393). Chicago, IL: University of Chicago Press.

INDEX

Page numbers followed by *t* or *f* refer to tables and figures on respective pages.